DEMOCRACY

IN

GERMANY

DD 259.2
.E69 D

THE JODIDI LECTURES
AT HARVARD UNIVERSITY

The Jodidi Lectures are made possible by the Samuel L. Jodidi and Elizabeth Jodidi Fund, established at Harvard University in 1955, to foster tolerance and understanding among nations. They are delivered under the auspices of the Center for International Affairs.

DEMOCRACY

IN

GERMANY

FRITZ ERLER

HARVARD UNIVERSITY PRESS

CAMBRIDGE · MASSACHUSETTS

1965

Library of Congress Catalog Card Number: 65–16683

Printed in the United States of America

Foreword

By Franklin L. Ford

Dean of the Faculty of Arts and Sciences,
Harvard University

On March 24, 1964, I had the honor of introducing Mr. Fritz Erler to an audience in Harvard's Sanders Theater for the first of his three Jodidi Lectures. Earlier that same evening, through the kindness of Professor Robert Bowie, director of our Center for International Affairs and immediate sponsor of the lectures, we had had a chance to dine and to talk at leisure. Some dinners preceding formal speeches are pretty stiff affairs, and some are downright joyless. This one, thanks to Mr. Erler, was nothing of the kind.

The speaker of the evening turned out to be a stockily built man in his early fifties, soberly dressed, balding and bespectacled — at first glance the very figure of responsible opposition in the German Federal Republic. But Mr. Erler, it takes only a few moments of conversation to discover, is an extraordinary man. His judgments are shrewd, his characterizations are pungent, and woven into his polite discourse is a kindly wit, welcome in any man and truly amazing in one who has suffered through some of his nation's darkest and most brutal days. The engaging dinner table companion proved to be an equally arresting lecturer, to whom, for three consecutive

evenings, Harvard audiences listened with close attention. Now the text of his remarks, revised and expanded,
fortunately becomes available to a wider audience. But
more of the book in a moment.

First, let me add a few words about the author. Born
into a Berlin workman's family in 1913, he grew up in
the Social Democratic youth organizations of the Weimar
Republic. When Hitler came to power, such movements,
if they survived at all, necessarily went underground,
and by 1935 Erler was the twenty-two-year-old leader of
one of them, the "Neu Beginnen," working in secret
opposition to the National Socialist government. In 1938
he was arrested and convicted of treason. For seven years
thereafter he was a prisoner of the Nazis, only to escape
in 1945 when a prison train which was transferring him
from one jail to another was not properly guarded at
night. As a result of this uncommonly happy incident,
two inmates scrambled to freedom.

Erler's career in the politics of post-Hitlerian Germany
began in a quite standard way, but shortly became remarkable. After working briefly for the administration
of the French Zone of Occupation, he was named *Landrat*
(or District Commissioner) of Tuttlingen, a pleasant
town in southern Württemberg, where the nascent Dan-
ube comes down out of the Black Forest. Elected to the
first Bundestag of the new Federal Republic in 1949, he
moved his political activity to Bonn; but despite exten-
sive travels, he has made the city of Pforzheim in his
constituency his home ever since. As parliamentary floor
leader of the Social Democrats, he obviously occupies a
national political post of critical significance. As West

Germany's chief delegate to the Council of Europe and
as a member of the Western European Union, he just as
obviously looms large in the international councils of
the old, resurgent continent. Finally, he stands immediately below Willy Brandt, his party chairman, in the
structure of the SPD, or Social Democrats, and has
sometimes been referred to as the Social Democrats'
"shadow foreign minister."

In these lectures on German democracy, Mr. Erler
recounts a good deal of history. He does not add to our
store of facts — and such was not his aim. Instead, he
offers a valuable explication of what a present-day German of his background and current responsibilities makes
of the century's most tormented national record. Simply
as a personal statement, therefore, the historical com-
mentary is a valuable document, and as such, I am sure,
it will be thoughtfully studied. For me at least, the good
sense and the good will which inform his conclusions
are deeply reassuring.

But quite aside from the documentary value of Mr.
Erler's remarks, we can perceive in them another level
of importance. These are the words, carefully weighed,
at times surprisingly candid, of a key figure within Germany's "other party," one of the potential leaders of a
future West German government. Devout as most of us
Americans are with respect to our own two-party system,
and ready as we have generally been to recognize the
need for good communication not only with the Government but also with the Opposition, in the case of
Great Britain, for example, we have shown ourselves
surprisingly slow to recognize, either officially or un-

officially, the equivalent need with respect to Germany. At times during the German general election campaigns of 1949, 1953, and 1957 (though happily to nowhere the same degree in 1961), some spokesmen for the United States appeared to believe that America and Chancellor Adenauer's Christian Democratic Union were running for election hand in hand.

To suggest that this was unfortunate is not to detract in the least from the achievements of Adenauer, Erhard, Brentano, Schroeder and other leading Christian Democrats — any more than our government's present readiness to do business with Prime Minister Wilson is a repudiation of the high value it previously put on close understandings with Prime Ministers Macmillan and Home. The fact is that the Social Democrats now are in a position to take their turn from time to time in the control of West German policy. It thus behooves us to give the SPD's leadership and its views some mature consideration. Willy Brandt's emergence into prominence several years ago induced us to begin that overdue exercise. The ensuing pages by Fritz Erler should carry us several stages further.

CONTENTS

TABLES

DEMOCRACY
IN
GERMANY

→» **1** «←

Question Marks

In traveling through the United States, a visitor from Germany is very often drawn into a discussion on the past, the present, and the future of his country. Two world wars in which Germany and the United States fought against each other have left many sad memories. As a consequence of the dreadful Hitler regime, thousands of German Jews, persecuted intellectuals, and other Europeans from countries under German occupation sought shelter in America and started a new life there. What they had to tell of the reign of terror which drove them from Europe and which killed millions of their kinsmen and countrymen was and is not apt to create a wave of sympathy for the German nation.

Some twenty years have passed since the war ended. For the younger generation, this seems to be a long time. In the memories of those who lived through the 1930's and 1940's, however, and of course in the life of nations and of mankind as a whole, it is but a very short span. In this short span, astonishing changes have occurred. For nearly ten years now, Germany and the United States have been allies cooperating within the framework of NATO in order to preserve peace, freedom, and democracy. The World War II alliance between the U.S.A. and the Soviet Union, formed to combat Hitler's aggression, was already shaky as Germany's defeat approached. That alliance broke down definitely when it became clear that the Soviet Union and the Western partners in the alliance had contradictory conceptions of the future of Germany and of Europe. But this course of events is seen more clearly through hindsight than it was seen at the time. The present alignment of world forces is a long way removed from the original conflict of interests between the wartime allies.

An abrupt historical movement has in fact led to a complete *renversement des alliances.* The free part of Germany, the Federal Republic of Germany, has become an important member of the European Communities, of the Atlantic Alliance, and of international organizations serving various purposes. The part of the country under Soviet occupation is run by a Communist puppet government without popular support. It is actually a Soviet colony in Central Europe. Its captive citizens regard the Federal Republic of Germany as their spokesman as long as they cannot speak for themselves. They want a democratic Germany — not a Communist one.

These important international developments are of course well known, but the German visitor to the United States is often questioned about his country's internal stability and national state of mind. Is the new democratic state really more stable than the Weimar Republic, which was so quickly destroyed and followed by the Hitler regime? In the 1920's the world was told that

Germany had built a democratic framework of society which would never give way to fascism as Italy had given way to Mussolini, who between 1922 and 1925 made himself dictator by force. And then was not just that type of government imposed on Germany with even more cruelty, perfection, and efficiency? What kind of spirit prevails at present? What kind of armed forces, government organization, political parties, schools, and pressure groups? What safeguards open brighter prospects for democracy in Germany now than between the two world wars?

These are pertinent questions. They are the more understandable when we read in the papers that men responsible for terrible crimes during the Hitler period or at least during the war could escape from prison and meet in Egypt, where former German scientists work in Nasser's war industry directed against Israel. We read also that certain trials do not lead to sentences corresponding to the crimes committed, that certain newspapers and politicians ask for a general amnesty in order to end these trials once for all, and that other newspapers try to boost sales by publishing illustrated stories about Hitler and his companions. There are still people in official positions who held high offices under Hitler. New investigations — very often set off by the carefully calculated and well-timed publication of documents by the Eastern European governments or by the Communist authorities in the Soviet Zone of Germany — again and again uncover people in the police, in the judiciary, and in other state positions who were involved in criminal or important political activities of the Nazi regime. And sometimes we read that gravestones in Jewish burial grounds have been defaced, and that Nazi symbols and slogans reappear on the walls.

Do such events foreshadow the return of a totalitarian regime in Germany? Or do they represent a diminishing part of the dreadful past in Germany's present, more than compensated by institutions, ideas, men, and forces working for the good cause?

This book is not able to give an impartial, scientific answer to that query. It is written not by a scholar but by a man who is proud to have his part in the actual political effort to maintain democracy in Germany. Therefore this book is not entirely free from partisan views, but it tries to describe developments and facts we should know if we want to reach a fair judgment. There is nothing really new in the book. An amazing number of analytical studies have been written on modern Germany. Nevertheless, it is perhaps useful to group some of the facts around certain important questions and to add some views gained from the experience of a man who did not merely reflect on the latest chapters of German history but who suffered and lived them through in changing capacities.

THE DISTANCE FROM BONN TO WEIMAR

Let us describe first the main differences between the Federal Republic of Germany and the Weimar Republic of 1918 to 1933. The new republic cannot be separated from the German past, but neither is it just a second edition of the Weimar state. Undoubtedly, its political structure is more stable. This greater stability results in part from the lessons the political leaders of modern German democracy have drawn out of the history of their nation, in part from the greater solidarity and encouragement the Western democracies have shown to their new German sister, and in part from the over-all political and economic situation of Western Europe since World War II.

The Bonn constitution, fifteen years old on May 23, 1964, takes effective precautions against that form of governmental instability from which the Weimar state suffered so severely.* Only political parties polling more than 5 per cent of the total votes cast or winning at least three constituencies by a relative majority (being the strongest party there) are represented in the federal Parliament (Bundestag). Similar rules apply to the state parliaments (Landtage). This has led to the disappearance of all splinter parties from the federal Parliament and from most of the state parliaments. The voter does not want to throw away his vote for nothing. He wants representation. This system has therefore created a concentration of the electorate on the two large parties, the Christian Democrats (CDU), under the leadership of former Chancellor Konrad Adenauer, and the Social Democrats (SPD), with Mayor Willy Brandt of Berlin as chairman in succession to the late Erich Ollenhauer and Dr. Kurt Schumacher. Among smaller groups, only the Free Democrats (FDP), led by Dr. Erich Mende,

* A serviceable English translation of the Bonn constitution, amended through 1961, appears in *The Basic Law of the Federal Republic of Germany* (New York: German Information Center, n.d.). All quotations from the Bonn constitution used in this book are taken from that source.

have succeeded in holding a place in a Bundestag where 90 per cent of the seats are now held by the two large parties.* Even such important groups as the refugees and expellees are no longer represented by a special party of their own on the federal level. Their organization, Gesamt-Deutsche Partei, has also lost most of its representation in the Landtage. The refugee part of the population in West Germany, amounting to more than 25 per cent of the electorate, has been integrated in the general political structure and has found its place with the rest of the citizenry in the great parties.

All this has been achieved without introducing the British system whereby only one direct representative for each constituency is elected by a relative majority there. Discussions about adopting that system take place in Germany now and then. But, with good cause, the Free Democrats are opposed to it, fearing for their political survival, and others fear the predominance in seats that the system might give to the strongest party. It would work fairly only if no party were favored officially by one of the great churches.

The electoral system in West Germany is in fact based on proportional representation. One half of the federal Parliament is chosen by the relative majority in each of the 248 constituencies, and the other half is named from party lists in such a way that the total representation of

* The German names of these three parties are: Christlich-Demokratische Union (CDU), Sozialdemokratische Partei Deutschlands (SPD), and Freie Demokratische Partei (FDP). The Bavarian wing of the CDU is called Christlich-Soziale Union (CSU); on a federal level the CDU and CSU act practically as one party, and they form one group in the federal parliament, but the CSU claims a certain independence as a separate regional party.

a party in Parliament is proportional to its share in the total votes of the country, once the party has passed the 5 per cent limit.

Something of the spirit which guides political parties under the Bonn Republic may be judged from a subarticle in the constitution that specifically states: "Their internal organization must conform to democratic principles." Other constitutional provisions which improve upon the Weimar experience give the Bundestag the right to hold public hearings, with legal and administrative assistance, and to maintain watchdog committees during the interval between legislative terms.

Another important innovation was the introduction of the so-called constructive censure vote. As in pre-Gaullist France, temporary majorities in the Weimar legislature could easily overthrow the executive, and they often did so. The Bonn system requires Parliament to elect a new executive in removing the old one. Only by installing a new chancellor to carry on the nation's business can Parliament turn a former chancellor out of office. This gives an extraordinary stability and continuity to the executive branch. Artificial coalitions of the extreme right and left (and none has existed in the Bundestag in a decade) are prevented from causing chaos. At the same time, a change in the composition of the executive and of the governing majority remains possible if the political situation or personal problems make this desirable. The Federal Republic of Germany is a parliamentary democracy, not a presidential regime.

The Bonn system has already accommodated a change of chancellors with relative ease — when Dr. Ludwig

Erhard succeeded Dr. Adenauer in 1963. This of course happened without a change of majority party and without a censure vote. The former chancellor resigned; a new one was elected. But the system functioned, and in a way one could not count on in Weimar days.

A German government must have the confidence of Parliament. The chief executive does not serve a fixed term as in the United States. The chancellor has some of the freedom of the American president in running his cabinet. Parliament can criticize ministers but not expel them from the cabinet by a vote. The head of government can keep a minister who is attacked. Should feeling against a minister run so high, however, as to threaten the constructive censure vote against the chancellor, cabinet members are vulnerable. This explains why a very strong combination of pressure from the opposition, public opinion, and important parts of the government coalition itself, but only such a combination, can cause the fall of a minister. Such was the case of former Minister of Defense Franz-Josef Strauss in 1962 and of former Minister for Refugees Theodor Oberländer in 1960.

The Bonn constitution has concentrated executive powers on the head of government, the chancellor, and sharply circumscribed the powers of the president of the Federal Republic of Germany, its head of state. The president, as the symbol of national unity, should not take part in the struggle between the political parties. He is elected for five years by a special federal convention (Bundesversammlung) consisting of the federal Parliament and the same number of representatives elected by the state parliaments. His authority is more a

moral than a legal one. He appoints, on the recommenda-
tion of the government, the more important civil servants
and military officers. He signs the laws passed by Parliament and publishes them. After general elections, he
proposes his candidate for chancellor to the Bundestag.
But Parliament can refuse this proposal and elect another
candidate.

The president has no far-reaching emergency powers
such as his predecessor claimed in the Weimar Republic.
There is no equivalent to the infamous Article 48 of the
Weimar constitution, used so often for legislation when
Parliament was paralyzed, misused in July, 1932, by von
Papen in smashing Prussia's democratic government, and
then exploited in 1933 to confer tremendous powers for
terror and oppression on Hitler.

Legislation for emergency cases is now under consideration in Germany. Article 48 is not forgotten; its grisly
ghost hangs over the discussion of the proposed new law.
General agreement has been expressed that both Parliament and the executive must remain accountable. No
elected body is likely again to be allowed to desert its
responsibilities by leaving action to the president, who
himself is *not* responsible to Parliament. The power to
move quickly may be desirable for modern governments,
but not to the detriment of the constitution. These are
the lessons drawn by the Social Democrats from the
experience with Article 48 of the Weimar constitution.
Their resistance to the emergency law (*Ermächtigungs-
gesetz*) of March 1933 is well known. They feel confirmed
in their position by the events that followed after July
1932, and after the decision of the Reichstag majority in

1933. There will only be emergency legislation in West Germany if the necessary precautions against possible misuse are taken. Any amendment to the Bonn constitution requires a two-thirds majority. Therefore it cannot pass against the SPD — the Social Democrats.

Finally, under the Bonn system the president is *not* the high commander of the armed forces. This stems from the fact that he does not carry any responsibility to Parliament. The civilian, responsible government holds ultimate command of the Bundeswehr, to ensure its use only in accordance with the will of chancellor and Parliament, never without or against it. "The numerical strength and general organizational structure of the Armed Forces raised for defense by the Federation," says Article 87a of the Bonn constitution, "shall be shown in the budget." This is new for Germany and, together with other legislation related to this point, has far-reaching consequences.

CHECKS AND BALANCES

Democracy in West Germany has found a set of checks and balances other than that of the German past. For one thing, federalism has become a very important feature. When the new constitution was discussed by the *Parlamentarischer Rat* in 1948 and 1949, the Western Allies exercised their influence in the debates. But it is doubtful that the outcome would have been very different had the Allies not expressed their wishes. When, for example, strong opposition to a plan for limiting federal power to a kind of weak confederation was marshaled by the Social Democratic leader, Dr. Kurt

Schumacher, the Allies yielded. And the mechanism of federalism has worked. Centralization is easier and in some matters more popular. But the participation of the states — in a second chamber, called the Bundesrat, which is composed of representatives of the state governments — in federal lawmaking has avoided many clashes and given the benefit of the administrative experience of the states to the federal government. It has also gained for the SPD, which is in power in five of the eleven states, a higher amount of participation in federal affairs than that which would result only from its function as the opposition party in the Bundestag.

Of course, this type of federalism has its problems. There is great disparity between the school systems of the various states, for example. Children coming from one region to another find it difficult to adjust to schools following a different program in languages and so on. To bring about more cooperation without centralization is a difficult task. But the existence and the power of the states put limits to a possible misuse of power by the federal government. This was evident when the government tried to create a new television network under its financial and political control. This attempt failed because some state governments sued the federal government successfully before the Constitutional Court.

This court, too, is an innovation in German history. "All state authority emanates from the people," says Article 20 of the Bonn constitution. "It is exercised by the people by means of elections and voting and by separate legislative, executive, and judicial organs. Legislation is subject to the constitutional order; the executive and the judiciary are bound by the law." The court's judges are not appointed by the government but are elected by a mixed committee of Bundestag and Bundesrat. Its judicial independence has won the confidence of the country. The citizen knows that chancellor and Parliament have to respect the constitution. The fact that in important political cases laws have had to be modified and governmental actions nullified gives to the court not only esteem but strength to become even more independent. Of course, the stream of political events has to be channeled through elections and the other branches of government. A Constitutional Court alone cannot save democracy against the will or the inertia of the nation. In a real conflict between power and justice, justice is always in danger. But the court has contributed to such a healthy separation of powers and to such respect for law that better prospects of avoiding such a conflict now exist.

Hand in hand with the makers of the present German constitution, the political parties as such have drawn some lessons from the past and introduced new practices that augur well for the future. They support the state rather than work for its collapse as the strong antirepublican forces on the Conservative right and the Communist left did in Weimar days. At that time there was in the very democratic parties themselves occasionally only a lukewarm response to parliamentary democracy. The political fight has become more civilized now. There are still truculent speeches and misuses of state power for party purposes. But the common ground between the parties is much larger than in the past. Although the

Social Democratic opposition may not be conceived as a possible alternative government by everybody, the idea that opposition can be legitimate and constructive has taken hold in recent years.

The disappearance of extremists is a striking feature. There are small firebrand groups, but they are without influence. Not only the 5 per cent clause but also the general economic, social, and political developments have worked against them. The direct successors to the Hitler party are outlawed by a decision of the Constitutional Court, as is the Communist Party. The constitution in Article 18 gives the court leeway to deprive those parties of political rights which threaten to deny them to others upon accession to power. Quite possibly, however, the government erred in starting legal proceedings against such groups when they would have failed utterly at the polls. The ruling against Communists, for example, gives them the undeserved crown of martyrs. But elections prior to court action had shown their losses. In free elections they would not poll today in the Federal Republic much more than the 1 per cent they get in West Berlin, where the party continues to exist under cover of the four-power status for the whole of Berlin (which did not save the democratic parties from persecution in East Berlin).

WESTERN SUPPORT

The solidarity of the Western democracies with Germany has contributed very much to the healthy development. The nation has not forgotten the economic and political help by the U.S.A. after World War II. The

Marshall Plan, Organization for European Economic Cooperation (OEEC), and the European Communities have played an important part in the rebuilding of the German economy. The difference between the rest of Germany and the Soviet Zone is striking. American military strength has provided the largest part of our defense against Soviet pressure. Berlin remained free by a common effort of the Western powers, West Germany, and the Berlin population. The blockade of that city in 1948 and the victory over it created strong emotional links between the free parts of Germany and the West. Furthermore, it was the West that brought the Federal Republic of Germany into a series of international organizations on the basis of equal rights prior to the acceptance of Germany as an ally in NATO. All this is remarkably different from the wavering of the Western powers between equality and discrimination, understanding and isolation, confidence and mistrust in the Weimar period.

Soviet policy has helped to further democracy in Germany. The experience with Soviet occupation and Communist rule has contributed as much to a certain immunization against totalitarianism as did the terrible Nazi chapter of bloodshed, crime, and shame in the annals of the nation. Soviet pressure on Berlin, Soviet policy for perpetuating the division of the country, and Soviet psychological warfare against the Germans as being the eternal warmongers, the one aggressive and militarist nation on the globe, keep the Germans disgusted with militant ideology. Insofar as the Western powers resisted these pressures and corrected these distortions of the truth, the democratic forces in Germany were encouraged and strengthened by the proof of solidarity. No one is more aware than the Germans that just that part of Germany where the Soviet Union is in command shows most resemblance to Nazi totalitarianism, with its police control, paranoiac military displays, and drive against the churches.

ECONOMIC RESURGENCE

In gauging the present stability of democracy in Germany, we should not underestimate the economic and social situation. With the help of the West, a great common effort has created an expanding economy in Germany. Ruins and misery and the influx of more than 12 million refugees and expellees were the basis for a nearly unlimited economic demand. Trained manpower, the will to recover, foreign aid, the U.S.-sponsored currency reform, and the initiative of government, business, and labor helped to create what later was called the "economic miracle."

West Germany not only enjoys full employment but also attracts labor from abroad. About 800,000 workers from foreign countries have found jobs there in recent years. The wage level has reached a high level, remaining behind the U.S.A. and Sweden but approximating that of most other Western industrialized countries. Full employment and the moderate policy of the trade unions permitted the pay scale to rise with relatively little loss of production through strikes. The existence of strong unions and a strong social democratic party stirred the governing majority party to modernize German social legislation in many important fields. Much remains to be done but the social structure of West Germany today is far removed from nineteenth-century capitalism.

This is recognized by the unions, not least because their own activities have very much contributed to the present state of affairs. The unions are strongholds for democracy in West Germany. Naturally they criticize things which do not please them and they often ask for more concessions than business and the present government are ready to grant. But they know that only a free society has room for free unions, that every totalitarian regime starts with destroying the freedom of the unions in order to control the labor force. Therefore, the unions are even more cautious than the SPD in regard to emergency laws. They are zealous guardians of the right to strike, of freedom of association, and of welfare programs.

The SPD tries to shape legislation in such a way as to meet the aspirations and alleviate the worries of the unions, whose democratic record is impressive. Several times after 1918 they carried out political strikes to save democracy. Their strikes against the excessive dismantling of industry in Germany after 1945 were welcomed by the same business community which now seems to have forgotten these events. Any provision for emergency powers should give a positive role to the unions. In case of danger for German democracy, its loyal supporters, the unions, must be activated, not damaged.

PEACEFUL CHANGE

We do not know whether German democracy would remain stable if it were put under strain by an economic depression, by political isolation from the West, or, even worse, by a combination of the two. But governments have learned how to handle economic problems better since the early 1930's and since John Maynard Keynes. German economic policy is much more flexible than the somewhat dogmatic speeches of Chancellor Erhard make believe. For the sake of the future of democracy, no German government can dare to write off full employment, whatever the proclaimed economic theories might be. And every responsible political party in Germany is aware of the necessity of the closest possible links with the Western democracies. There are some who envisage perhaps a Europe modeled on Gaullist lines, with more political distance from England and the U.S.A. Their concept is based on a more authoritarian view of leadership and on skepticism about the present version of parliamentary democracy. But they do not by any means want German isloation or unilateral negotiation with the Soviet Union. It means much to the cause of democracy in Germany for the West to maintain its solidarity and continue to regard the Federal Republic as a reliable friend.

To survive, democracy must provide for accommodation and peaceful change in place of revolutionary disturbances, and the Federal Republic of Germany has still to stand that test in the field of parliamentary power. Since her birth, she has been governed by the Christian Democrats, alone or in a coalition with smaller partners. A one-party system is incompatible with a democratic future. If and when a change in the ruling party will take place is up to the electorate to decide. Meanwhile, the stronger the opposition party becomes, the more the party in power is tempted to use the apparatus of the state in favor of the party. Germany has no tradition of the transfer of power between the two great parties, as the U.S.A. and Great Britain have. But the internal development of the Social Democratic Party, the larger amount of respect it has earned among those parts of the population who were very hostile, the credit the party enjoys abroad for its firm stand for democracy in very critical times, and a growing understanding of the normal character of such a change — all lead to the hope that this proof of a democratic standard will be given by Germany too.

⇮ 2 ⇮

Years of Desperation

GERMANY IS NOT without honorable democratic traditions of long standing. What we would now call the first Landtag (state parliament) met as early as November 7, 1457, in Württemberg in the southwest part of Germany. A present-day German visitor to Williamsburg, Virginia, as he examines the building occupied by the first Virginia assembly, has the feeling that the American colonial assemblies were shaped in a very similar way to councils like that of Württemberg. Germany put forth more or less democratic constitutions in the large cities of the Hanseatic League. In the nineteenth century, German resistance against Napoleon was paired with demand for domestic reform. The Prussian army was reformed, the peasants were liberated, and local self-government was granted.

Since that time, municipal life has been the real training ground for democratic government in Germany. Local government developed many initiatives and step by step won more authority in relation to the central state. When the right to vote was no longer limited to property holders, other groups joined in, exercising their rights and learning responsibilities. It is no surprise that after the breakdown of government in 1945, the reconstruction of democratic life in Germany started from the bottom, in the towns and cities. There, the surviving elements of the old democratic parties appeared again on the scene and formed the now existing political parties. In rapid order, state-wide and nation-wide parties were formed which were able to form elected bodies that replaced the authorities appointed provisionally by the occupying powers.

The grant of self-government in the nineteenth century was followed by a long fight for constitutions and the fight for national unity within what had been the old German Empire and since 1815 the German Confederation. All this together made the grandeur and failure of the Revolution of 1848. Germany did not get a unified democratic state through the Revolution of 1848. Instead, Bismarck made his state by blood and iron. He fulfilled the national aspirations for unity under the leadership of Prussia, in whose interests he excluded the German-speaking parts of Austria. We have to add that Bismarck introduced for the first time free, general, and direct secret elections. That was a great achievement, if it was compared with the past; but it was not enough, because the Parliament of the whole of Germany, the Reichstag in Berlin, had little power. The imperial government was responsible not to Parliament but to the emperor.

In the latter part of the nineteenth century, new democratic forces organized themselves. The SPD was founded a century ago; the trade unions came into existence; and the Catholic church favored a labor movement, though not of the social democratic type. The Protestant church, however, was somewhat reserved and hostile. It was linked too closely with the throne. The Kaiser was at the same time the highest bishop of the Protestant church. With this social structure Germany came into World War I, partly through her own designs, partly through the schemes and blunders of other powers. Many mistakes on all sides had led to that catastrophe, and in the end Germany was defeated. The Kaiser left the country. The old authority broke down. The Revolution of 1918 brought a serious attempt at creating parliamentary democracy on German soil — the Weimar Republic.

UNPOPULAR DEMOCRACY

The Weimar Republic suffered from the very beginning the onus of being identified with a national defeat, but, even aside from that, the new state aroused no patriotism. Perhaps this is a result of the fact that the Germans never killed a king. Other nations won the feeling of self-government by doing this. The Germans never did it. As was mentioned, the Kaiser left them. In 1918 and 1919, the new state had to fulfill some very important tasks. Under the leadership of Social Democrats like Friedrich Ebert and Gustav Noske, the new authorities had to preserve the unity of the state against separatist sedition on different sides, had to establish parliamentary democracy in the face of attempts by the Communists to transfer the Russian Revolution to German soil, had to organize free elections at the risk of themselves losing office. Immediately afterwards the Social Democratic Party had to share power with others and later even to give it up.* Who, then, supported wholeheartedly the new democratic republic? Unfortunately, not the majority of the nation. There were active enemies on the right and the left. Active minorities in the Social Democratic Party tended to regard the new republic as only a kind of transition to what they believed a socialist state should be. The great majority of the nation was not much interested at all.

The difficulties were compounded by some mistakes of the Western Allies during those years. There was no commitment from the United States to Europe. The United States refused to enter the League of Nations even after Weimar Germany had become a member, a step which the Social Democrats had advocated for years against the arguments of the conservatives. There was still discrimination against the defeated enemy.

Germany was in a poor position to make the reparations demanded of her. For a while they were offset by

* The Weimar Republic began under the Social Democratic chancellorship of Philipp Scheidemann. Between February 1919 and January 1933, no less than nineteen separate administrations were formed, all of them including ministers from more than one party and several of them simultaneously including ministers with no party affiliation. This does not begin to indicate the chaos, however, for the ideological shifts were as extreme as the frequency of change. Three successive governments were in power during 1920, for example. Two of them were led by Social Democratic chancellors, but the third, with Konstantin Fehrenbach as chancellor and the so-called Center Party and National Liberals predominating, excluded the Social Democrats entirely. Then, after occupying no ministerial posts whatever in seven of the next ten governments, the Social Democrats put Hermann Müller in as chancellor in 1928. When his government fell in 1930, the number of conservatives increased in succeeding government coalitions, and the Social Democrats never took office again under the Weimar Republic.

American credits. But disaster came when, in the time of the world depression, the credits were withdrawn. The German economy collapsed. There was a good deal of reconstruction until 1929. Then came the world crisis. The Allied powers made only minor concessions on national problems to the Weimar Republic. They conceded far more later to the blackmailing Hitler. This did not strengthen the democratic forces in Germany.

The hopeless economic situation after 1930, with a deflation policy running contrary to the theories of Keynes which were just then being grasped as a way to recovery, led to mass unemployment. Counting the families of those out of work, roughly one third of the population experienced unemployment. Many of the unemployed, as well as debt-ridden farmers and intellectuals, refused to support the republic.

Strangely enough, this period, so bad in other ways, was a time of great cultural achievements, the results of which can still be seen. The arts, theater, architecture, and literature flourished. Later, when Hitler started persecution against nearly all the intellectual parts of the population, refugees poured into the United States and contributed to cultural life there. After World War II many of their ideas, coming this time from America, influenced a Germany which had refused to accept them before.

That the nation was hostile to its own cultural achievements in the 1920's may perhaps be blamed on the educational system. This was very traditionalist. Moreover, the armed forces were separated from civil life. They were not under political control. The president of the republic was high commander, but he had no responsibility toward Parliament. Thus characteristics of monarchy had been transferred to the president. The situation of the armed forces did not destroy democracy, but it did not help. There was no inner relation between the armed forces and the democratic state. The armed forces felt as though they were the real state, and they looked with a kind of contempt on Parliament and political parties and elections in general as childish toys. This was partly the result of the fact that soldiers had neither the right to vote nor to be a candidate.

After 1930 there was no longer a majority in Parliament which wanted Weimar Germany to survive. The extremists of left and right between them had a majority. Germany witnessed the start of an authoritarian rule, and in July 1932 came the downfall of the most important democratic fortress remaining in Germany, namely, the government of Prussia. It was demolished by Franz von Papen (who quite recently has been wholeheartedly welcomed as a lecturer by the present regime in Spain).

The question arises: why did the democratic forces, especially the Social Democrats and the trade unions, not show a more forceful resistance in 1932 toward that *coup d'état* of von Papen? One answer is that the unions doubted the effectiveness of a general strike in time of mass unemployment, and they also had doubts about the effectiveness of a strike when public opinion seemed overwhelmingly against them on political grounds. Germany has seen successful strikes in the political field — in defense of democracy in 1920 at the time of the Kapp *Putsch*, for example, and after the murder of the demo-

cratic foreign minister Walter Rathenau in 1922. The
majority sympathized with the strikers on those occasions,
however. Against widespread hostility, political resistance
by unions is difficult. And the Social Democrats, like the
unions, would not seek or accept support from the Communists, who in the Weimar period mustered a sizable
number of votes in the German labor force. Support from
the Communists was shunned because the Communists
did their best to destroy democracy. They proclaimed the
"united front of the working class" — but under their control and against the democratic parties and institutions.
In fact, they cooperated effectively with the Nazis. In the
plebiscite of August 9, 1931, for example, the Nazis, the
Conservatives, and the Communists together had attempted to overthrow the democratic Prussian government, consisting of a coalition of the Social Democrats,
the Democrats, and the (Catholic) Center. That first
attempt had failed. One could not expect that in 1932 the
Communists would defend the same government they
had tried to overthrow one year earlier. Even after von
Papen's *coup d'état*, this curious cooperation between the
extremists continued. Together they organized a wildcat
strike in the Berlin public transport system in November
1932. The Communists regarded the Social Democrats
as their most important enemies — they called them
"Social Fascists." They were convinced that a Hitler
regime would be a very short one out of which they
would rise to power. This was a cruel error. Even if in
the light of history the Communist regime in the Soviet
Zone of Germany were construed as the direct consequence of the policy of the Hitler era, what sufferings

had to be undergone toward that end! Nevertheless, one can argue that the democratic parties, the unions, and the police, at least locally in Berlin, might have been able to save the government of Prussia and thus perhaps give to history another trend. But it is fruitless to discuss this now. Perhaps there would have been some bloodshed, but less than later in World War II. The leaders of the Social Democrats estimated the situation differently on the basis of such information as they had.

It is a fact that Hitler in the critical year of 1932 did not command a majority. When President Hindenburg was elected against him, the vote was 53 per cent to 36.8 per cent. In the elections of November 1932, Hitler lost two million votes in relation to another election four months earlier. In January 1933 he won a little state election in a very small German province — approximately the size of Rhode Island — and there he swayed only 40 per cent of the electorate. (See Table 1.) Nevertheless, when Hindenburg decided to appoint him chancellor, that was the end of democracy. The last elections with more than one party on the ballot took place March 5, 1933. These elections were already heavily influenced by the massive wave of terror in the streets, by the first concentration camps, by the imprisonment of tens of thousands of Social Democrats, Communists, and other opponents, by the interdiction of critical newspapers, and by the monopoly on broadcasting held by Hitler's government.

An aroused population now looked forward with immense expectations to a regime that was thought to be able to change the economic situation, restore full employment, and uphold national honor. At the same time, Germany lived through a wave of terror after the burning of the Reichstag. It is not very important to know whether the building was really burned by some Nazi followers or by a foolish individual. What counts is the fact that the new regime used this fire as a marvelous pretext for abolishing civil rights and for starting all kinds of persecution and oppression. Hitler requested emergency powers from President Hindenburg and got them. Based on Article 48 of the Weimar constitution, the ordinance of February 28, 1933 (promulgated a few hours after the Reichstag burned!) wiped out political freedom. The press was put under control, most public meetings were forbidden, arrests were possible without a legal decision, and members of Parliament were arrested. The Nazi storm troopers (SA) assumed the role of auxiliary police and opened hundreds of their own centers of torture before the Secret State Police were created and took over that bloody business. The Nazis seized their victims under the hypocritical name of "protective arrest" (*Schutzhaft*), a device which lasted until the very end of the regime. And all this was done before the election. It was rather astonishing that even with their terrorism and their control of all the media of public information the Nazi Party won no majority but only 43.9 per cent of the votes. They were forced to form a coalition with the Conservatives, who had 8 per cent. The Social Democratic slogan "A vote for Hitler is a vote for War" made a certain impression but not enough. Most people did not believe it. They had to learn it the hard way later.

Hitler in his distorted theory of history subdivided

Table 1. Voting in the Final Days of the Weimar Republic

A. Hindenburg's Re-election as President of the Republic, 1932

	First round, March 13 (valid votes, 37,650,000)		Second round, April 10 (valid votes, 39,490,000)	
	Percentage of votes	Supported by	Percentage of votes	Supported by
Hindenburg	49.6	Center (Catholic); SPD (Social Democrats); DDP (Democrats); DVP (National Liberals); BVP (Bavarian People's Party)	53.0	Center; SPD; DDP; DNVP; BVP
Hitler	30.1	NSDAP (Nazis)	36.8	NSDAP; DNVP
Thälmann	13.2	KPD (Communists)	10.2	KPD
Duesterberg	6.8	DNVP (Conservatives)	…	….
Splinter candidates	0.3	….	…	….

B. Reichstag Elections, 1932 and 1933

Thousands of votes [a]

Parties	(1) Sixth Reichstag July 31, 1932	(2) Seventh Reichstag Nov. 6, 1932	(3) Eighth Reichstag Mar. 5, 1933	Percentage of votes (1)	(2)	(3)	Number of seats (1)	(2)	(3)
NSDAP	13,745.8	11,737.0	17,277.2	37.3	33.1	43.9	230	196	288
SPD	7,959.7	7,248.0	7,181.6	21.6	20.4	18.3	133	121	120

Center	5,782.0	5,325.2	5,498.5	15.7	15.0	14.0	97	90	92
KPD	5,282.6	5,980.2	4,848.1	14.3	16.9	12.3	89	100	81
DNVP	2,177.4	2,959.1	3,136.8	5.9	8.5	8.0	37	52	52
DVP	436.0	661.8	432.3	1.2	1.9	1.1	7	11	2
DDP	371.8	336.5	334.2	1.0	1.0	0.8	4	2	5
Splinter parties	1,127.0	1,224.1	634.7	3.0	3.2	1.6	11	12	7
Totals	37,162.1	35,759.1	39,655.0	100.0	100.0	100.0	608	584	647

C. Election in the State of Lippe, January 15, 1933

Parties	Votes	Percentage of votes	Seats	Votes in election of Seventh Reichstag, Nov. 6, 1932
SPD	29,827[b]	30.0	7	25,782
DVP	4,380	4.4	1	3,628
DNVP	6,013	6.1	1	9,414
KPD	11,040	11.1	2	14,601
NSDAP	39,065	39.6	9	33,038
EV (Protestant)	4,525	4.6	1	4,079
Splinter groups	4,089	4.2	0	.....

a Because of rounding, columns do not add exactly to totals.

b The Social Democrats drew 15 per cent more votes from Lippe as a whole in this election than in the previous election, and in the capital, Detmold, their support increased 25 per cent.

Sources: Part A, Statistisches Jahrbuch für das deutsche Reich, 1932, pp. 546, 547; Part B, same yearbook for 1933, pp. 539, 540; Part C, Wippermann, Deutscher Geschichtskalender, 1933, p. 78, except last column which is from Hauptergebnisse der Wahlen zum Reichstag am 6. November 1932, compiled in Büro des Reichswahlleiters, p. 23.

mankind into higher and lower nations, placing the blond, blue-eyed, northern part of the Germans on top. (He himself had not the slightest resemblance to this type.) His conception led to the most dreadful organized mass murder that mankind ever suffered. In critical times there is always a general search for scapegoats. In Hitler's Germany, the Jews were regarded as responsible for every evil. At other times in other places it has been the Catholics, or the Freemasons, or the Communists, or the Germans — this varies from place to place — but always there is a search for scapegoats. Responsibility never seems to lie within one's own group. Every dictatorial regime needs an enemy.* Hitler exploited the existing sentiments of hatred and frustration and gave them a superficial air of scientific legitimacy. He exploited old prejudices, much older than he himself was. The Catholic church, for example, only quite recently dropped from its textbooks a sentence that had nourished anti-Semitism over centuries. It is a revenge of history and a late triumph of Hitler's that many people now look on the German nation as many Germans looked on others before. The transplantation of a false assumption does not make it more true.

The tragedy of the decay of democracy in Germany in the 1920's and 1930's went beyond Hitler's twisted genius and had other and deeper roots. Ill-formed political and social institutions, authoritarian education in family, school, university, and armed forces, the existence

* Here a delightful remark that recently appeared in an English newspaper passes through my mind. It has little to do with the subject of this study, but I found it so enjoyable that I repeat it here: He who has a friend like De Gaulle does not need enemies any more.

of power without proper control, the lack of courage
and responsibility in the intellectual leadership of the
country, the many mistakes committed in the political
and economic field by leading individuals and political
parties — all this together had created a whole network
of evil. If we add to this the lack of understanding in
the Western democracies of the difficult fight of the
democratic forces in Germany and later the dreadful
consequences of the economic world crisis in that country, then we realize the complexity of the problem. In
those years desperation and vain hope incited millions
of men and women to give up freedom and to accept
bread and work and the promise of a glorious future in
exchange for tyranny. The germs of that disease exist
everywhere. The social and political framework of society determines whether these can spread or if the
healthy forces can develop enough antitoxins. Totalitarianism, the total command of a society by a well-organ-
ized minority, is a permanent danger of our time. It is no
German monopoly, as Fascist Italy, Communist Russia,
and other examples prove. The German type was so
specifically dreadful because it was combined with the
immense possibilities of a highly efficient industrial society. Even murder was industrialized. Once the ruthless
minority was in possession of the levers of command,
resistance — and there was resistance — became tantamount to suicide. Only a national catastrophe could
shake off the yoke.

THE ROAD TO WAR AND DEFEAT

On March 23, 1933, the new Reichstag gave Hitler
such broad "emergency" powers that he was no longer

obliged to ask them from the president. In fact, the constitution was abolished. There was no more separation of powers. The Reichstag had abdicated. The right to legislate had been transferred to the cabinet and its head who assumed later also the function of head of state and highest judge. Imprisonment and death penalties by the executive without reference to courts were maintained as a permanent instrument of policy. The states lost their rights and were transformed into provinces under the direct and unlimited control of the central government. On the basis of these powers, some months later the political parties were dissolved, if they did not dissolve themselves, as the center parties did. The ruling Nazi Party (NSDAP, or German National Socialist Worker's Party) was made a public corporation, not a state within the state but a party in control of state and society. Every attempt to form a political group outside that party or to reorganize one of the former parties was declared to be high treason and was savagely punished. The property and facilities which three generations of Social Democrats had created in their party buildings, newspapers, and printing offices were seized and given to Nazi organizations.

The fate of the trade unions was equally cruel. On May 2, 1933, their offices were occupied by storm troopers. Their names were given to organizations which cracked the whip over labor, clerical workers, and managers alike. This so-called German Work Front (DAF) acted as instrument of the Nazi Party to exercise political and economic control in every industrial plant, workshop, and office.

To complete this control over the nation, an attempt was made to bring the churches and the armed forces under direct party influence. In a hard struggle, the Protestant church kept its "independence," but only by proving its loyalty to the regime. Some parts of that church for a certain time fell under the control of Nazi fanatics. The Catholic church with its international hierarchy had a better chance. But the Catholics, too, had first to declare loyalty. Only later, when some of the mass crimes happened, did important church leaders rise in protest, not without result. The wave of terror in 1933 against the political left found both churches rather silent.

The armed forces, the Reichswehr, did not want to be brought under direct political control by the Nazi Party. But they sympathized generally with a policy that gave greater strength, more personnel, more money, and better equipment to Germany's military establishment. Therefore their relative isolation from the government and the party did not very much disturb the new rulers. This isolation was favored by the continued exclusion of soldiers from such mock elections and political organizations as the Nazis permitted to exist, including the Nazi Party itself. Under cover of their exemption from "politics," army officers could easily refrain from revealing whether they agreed with the new regime or not. A tighter control was exercised only when, after some warnings about his adventurous foreign policy, Hitler in February 1938 dismissed some leading generals and reorganized the Reichswehr to his liking. Even then, the armed forces were a refuge for many men who, in serving there, avoided stronger pressure from the party. During the war, political officers were appointed to indoctrinate the armed forces and ensure their loyalty to Hitler. That action did not prevent the build-up of critical groups of officers who foresaw the inevitable defeat and therefore attempted a revolt in 1944. This was late but, for the honor and the future of the nation, better than never.

Keynes was never mentioned, but his policy was taken over in Germany by Hjalmar Schacht, Hitler's Minister of Economics. The period of re-employment of millions of people began, but also the very early stage of rearmament with hidden inflation, with an administered economy, with preparation for war. Step by step the Western powers yielded, giving us a common lesson we should conserve for today and tomorrow: that it does not pay to appease a blackmailing dictator. Yielding does not satisfy him; it whets his appetite. The introduction of conscription, the occupation of the Rhineland, the Treaty of Munich, and the destruction of Austria and Czechoslovakia did not prevent war. They hastened it, and in September 1939 we had it. A lot of cruelty had been shown in Germany before, and now it was shown outside Germany to all the countries which suffered from German occupation. The catastrophe at the end was unavoidable.

Clear-sighted men could see this in advance by calculating the power situation in the world, although the majority of the nation did not believe it. There was a minority resistance in Germany. Many of those who had fought against the Nazi movement before 1933 continued to do so in 1933 and later. The efficient terror of police and party, however, largely broke that resistance in 1933 and 1934. June 30, 1934, saw a terrible purge in the

Nazi movement itself. By order of Hitler, a number of leading storm troopers were killed by SS (*Schutzstaffeln*) units, Hitler's special guards in those years. (Later, the SS had a very diversified composition: political units at home, normal police units transferred to the SS, special units to guard and administer the concentration camps, and a large number of military units recruited among very young volunteers and even draftees and serving as "honor" divisions in the most dangerous sectors of the battle lines of World War II.) The purge of 1934 gave Hitler a splendid occasion to get rid of hundreds of political opponents, leading Catholic civil servants, former members of other parties, and influential intellectuals. But all the bloodshed and persecution did not prevent new groups of Germans from engaging in clandestine activity against Hitler. Greater experience and harder pressure generated new methods in smaller groups with less written or printed material. When such a group was caught, especially if it had contacts abroad, the sentences became harder and harder, the cases of capital punishment multiplying. So thousands of Germans had been killed and tens of thousands imprisoned in concentration camps before the occupation of other countries by Germany filled the cruel camps with victims from other nations.

The great sacrifices of the internal German resistance against an inhuman regime did not arouse a great deal of support from public opinion abroad. In France, for example, one could hear in 1934 and even 1937 that it was a good thing for the Germans now to have full employment, an efficient government, no more strikes, disciplined labor — and good that the Communists were outlawed. All this pleased some neighboring countries. Hitler got the benediction of respectable powers, led by the Vatican, which made a treaty with him in 1933. The impression was created at home that those who resisted Hitler fought against their own people, their own nation, rather than against a dictatorial regime. In fact, of course, they fought for all the real interest and honor of the nation. But it was very difficult to explain this. As time went on, the resistance got smaller in terms of the number of participants but much broader in social background, because a good many people joined that activity who had tolerated or even supported Hitler before. We know now of churchmen, soldiers, diplomats, and politicians — from the Conservatives to the Communists — who formed small circles hostile to a criminal regime. The Catholic priest Alfred Delp; the Protestant intellectual Dietrich Bonhoeffer; the Social Democrat member of Parliament Julius Leber; the former state minister Wilhelm Leuschner; the general Ludwig Beck; the former high-ranking civil servant Karl Goerdeler; the former Nazi police official Count von Helldorf; union leaders — these and many others wove the network of resistance which became visible July 20, 1944.

What if that movement had succeeded? Perhaps millions of people would have remained alive, fewer cities would have been destroyed, and the Soviet Union would not have entered Germany. Nobody knows. But the demand of unconditional surrender by the Western powers was not a good background for resistance activity in Germany. In the face of such a demand, the resistance, even if it won, could not hold out much of a prospect for the nation.

So came 1945, the defeat. The country was occupied and partitioned. Every occupation power tried to make out of its portion of Germany a kind of copy of the homeland. We had a little France, a little United States, a little England, and of course a little Russia. And this is the real story of the existing partition of Germany, because the Western powers introduced democracy, even though different forms. The differences between the former American, British, and French zones of occupation can still be seen in the police organization, the forms of local government, the teaching of languages, and so on. Since the Russians had no democracy at home, they introduced Communism. This was just the obvious result of the division of the country in zones. A complete change occurred in the social structure on the other side of the Iron Curtain. Originally, the Soviets had hoped that they could run a unified Germany from Berlin under Communist influence. I am convinced that this would have failed as it did in Austria. But Germany missed the chance. France rejected the establishment of certain German central administrations with a seat in Berlin under Allied control. The three Western powers subjected the population to a questionnaire about past activities and created democratic institutions in their parts of Germany. It was hard to do this without a revolution. To make a revolution by questionnaire is rather a difficult thing, and to introduce democracy by military government is a contradiction in itself. Therefore some difficulties had to be overcome. West Germany got the framework of her own democratic institutions with the aid, and sometimes against the opposition of, the Allies, but they grew.

The purge of former Nazis from administration and public life was undertaken in a somewhat clumsy way. Formalistic indications as to the length of membership, or the rank of the office held, served as a basis for decisions ranging from automatic arrest to dismissal from public service to fines or losses in income. The real responsibility of an individual for a certain part of the Nazi policy could not be found out by these procedures. Therefore these purges never were very popular in Germany — not because of sympathy with the Nazi leaders but because the procedure reminded many people of an assembly line in modern mass production. Satirists in the cabarets took the subject over, joking about the unimportant people who had to suffer while their one-time superiors more or less gained the protection of some Allied authorities through having a better command of foreign languages than the rank and file did.

This revolution-by-questionnaire reminded me of the treatment given to the American South after the Civil War. Such things sometimes have very far-reaching consequences. It looks as if the consequences of military occupation will not endure so long in Germany as they did and do in the United States.

The failure of that kind of "denazification" was the main reason that the reintegration of the personnel fired from public offices became inevitable. It was regarded as unfair that a lot of ordinary citizens should suffer more than others. Former professional soldiers complained bitterly at being outcasts. Not only were they excluded from exercising their former profession (which did not exist at all for ten years until 1955), but they were not admitted at universities for study and were debarred from certain jobs. This feeling of discrimination continues to exist even now when there is very little reason for it. Such are the scars from the first years after 1945.

In 1946, the first free elections were held, starting on the local level, then the state, and finally in 1949 the federal. After the currency reform in 1948, a new start was made in Germany's economic life. The development aid given to Germany in those years led to recovery and expansion more quickly than the aid she is now giving to others. The reason, of course, is that if there are trained people, one can rebuild faster. Investment in human knowledge and education takes more time than investment in machinery and buildings.

⇢≫ 3 ≪⇠

The Present Political Structure

CONTROVERSY WITHOUT CRISIS

For over a decade now West Germany has seen a hard fight between the political parties on social legislation, on fiscal measures, and on foreign policy. A good deal of personal animosity has been mixed in, but this is human and occurs in every country. That conflicts can be posed without undermining a basic consensus is a healthy sign.

All the main parties in West Germany stand firm on the ideological and practical ground of parliamentary democracy. There exists as in other democracies a pluralistic society with built-in checks and balances. But of course the German model is not exactly the same as that of others. The separation of power and the checks and balances in a federation are important. The different political parties check each other and therefore preserve the freedom of the citizen against the misuse of power by the party in power. West Germany has three main types of parties. The most progressive one is the Social Democratic Party, which could be compared to the liberal branch of the Democrats and the Republicans together in the U.S.A. Then there exists a more conservative party — the Christian Democrats. They resemble American Southern Democrats and the more conservative Republicans. The smallest of the three main parties is the Free Democratic Party. Its members label themselves liberal, but not in the American sense. Theirs is liberalism of the nineteenth century, with as little public responsibility for full employment and economic and social welfare as possible.

The press in West Germany is free. Competition exists between party papers and independent ones. Of course, the solicitation of advertising can create certain dependencies, and the government in office enjoys certain advantages in channeling information and expenditures. Therefore the character of the radio and television systems as independent corporations is a healthy corrective. As already mentioned, the attempt of the government to break that independence failed. The federal government lost that case before the Constitutional Court.

In a pluralistic society there are and must be independent interest groups such as labor and management. In collective bargaining both groups behave rather reasonably. West Germany loses fewer working hours through labor disputes than most other Western countries and yet enjoys a fair wage level and standard of living. More discipline in this respect exists only in the Scandinavian countries, in Holland, and in Switzerland, where strong social democratic parties and the trade unions recognize a common responsibility for full employment, economic growth, and social stability.

West Germany accommodates numerous voluntary associations and regulates them only to the extent that is considered necessary to protect society against hidden activities of extremist political organizations. There is complete freedom of organization of every kind and for every purpose, from sports to literature. It is therefore not surprising that the expellees and refugees have formed organizations to represent their interests. Since more than one quarter of the population of the Federal Republic of Germany is not native-born, these organizations are important in number and influence. But they are not equivalent to a special political party. Apparently the greater number of members of these organizations have tended to vote Christian Democratic. But a certain growth of Social Democratic influence is to be seen over the last years. It became manifest in the election of an SPD member of Parliament to the office of president of the association of expellees.

The large annual meetings of these organizations, when people from Pomerania meet in one city and those from the former German-speaking parts of Czechoslovakia (Sudetenland) in another, tend to raise suspicion and hostility abroad. It must be admitted that not all the speeches are tempered by statesmanship. The speech of Minister of Transport Hans-Christoph Seebohm on May 17, 1964, was officially rebuffed by the government, although this did not lead to Mr. Seebohm's being fired. But let us not forget that these millions of expellees had been forced to leave places where their ancestors had lived for centuries. They try to maintain personal contacts among themselves and to carry on the cultural heritage of their birthplace. Naturally they want a German government that will defend their legitimate interests when it comes to a peace conference on the definite future and size of Germany. They are impatient for a settlement. However, no responsible leader of these organizations ever advocated a settlement by force. Some of them try to envisage a future in which state boundaries would not have the same importance as today, when the East European nations will find a legitimate place in the developing European community. Europe does not end at the Iron Curtain. And all of them accept the *Charter of the German Expellees*, refusing violence, hatred, and revenge in claiming the right of self-determination as well as a fair peace settlement also for the entire German nation.* The influence of these organizations has been to moderate the demands of the refugee group. If this part of the population had not felt that they could express their concerns through the organizations, the birth of all kinds of extremist organizations would have been very likely.

Relations between government and opposition have still not reached the standard of an experienced democracy. Nevertheless the present opposition in Germany is

* The *Charter of the German Expellees*, signed by elected spokesmen of the various associations of refugees from former German-speaking areas, was proclaimed in the presence of government and church officials at Stuttgart on August 5, 1950, and subsequently endorsed at rallies in all parts of West Germany and published in several languages. "Almighty God himself placed men in their native land," says the charter. "We therefore feel competent," it says at another point, "to demand that the right to our native land be recognized . . . We do not, however, wish to stand aside and be doomed to inactivity, as long as this right is unrealized, but want, rather, to strive and toil with every member of our nation in a new spirit of community life, in a manner purified by a spirit of brotherly consideration."

not directed against the state. There was a period in German history when, really, the state was so reactionary, that the Social Democratic Party fought against it as well as the government of the day; but now it is quite clear that the SPD is part of the state, that it is striving only for a change in government. As is normal for every party, it wishes to come to power. It is fighting for social reform, not for revolution. Defamation of the opposition party as the enemy of the nation is no longer so common. And above all, this kind of defamation has lost credibility with the electorate. Former Chancellor Adenauer himself negotiated with the Social Democrats in the autumn of 1962 on a possible coalition. This destroyed a taboo. Those voters who were ardently in favor of other parties had to understand that the Social Democrats were regarded as capable of sharing responsibility in the federal government. The party itself was already convinced of that, of course. But now others had to recognize this, too. In a democratic society, all democratic parties must be regarded as possible partners in the government of the country. For democracy to work, no strong party can be regarded as an outcast forever.

Opposition holds open alternatives and makes a government account for its actions. There was a tendency in Germany, and perhaps is still, to say that there must be opposition but that the opposition should never come to power. Such a situation would destroy the healthy effect of the existence of an opposition. What is this effect? The opposition stands ready at any time the electorate chooses to launch the nation in new directions or correct abuses. The existence of such an opposition makes the government necessarily more cautious and responsible in using power. At the same time, the possibility of sharing power and coming to power has a healthy effect on the opposition itself. It cannot indulge in demagogic agitation, for promises can easily be compared to performance when the opposition party has come to power, and such comparison could lead to defeat in the next elections. Therefore the possibility of change in government is also a double safeguard of the freedom of the citizen against the misuse of power. If there is one hereditary party in power and one or more hereditary parties in the opposition, then there is no real democracy. If the same party is always in power, we would have to speak of a one-party system modified by a certain freedom of grumbling. Surely this is not the correct conception of democracy.

The lessons of German history do not apply only to the present Federal Republic of Germany. The other part of the country has not known freedom since 1933. Nevertheless, there is reason to hope for eventual freedom, because there is evidence that the people in the Soviet Zone have not been successfully indoctrinated by Communism. They carefully follow what is done in the larger part of the country. The face of the Communist part of Germany is very similar to the police state Germany has left behind her. It is the Communist edition of that same form of totalitarian society, but the difference is that this time the police state has no mass support, as was unfortunately the case with the Hitler regime. It has been created and protected only by foreign power. Even the young generation born and educated there after Hitler came to power has not given its allegiance to the Soviet-directed regime. More than 50 per cent of the German refugees who in the last ten years came from the other side of the Iron Curtain had not yet reached the age of twenty-five. With an average annual rate of roughly 300,000 refugees, the Communist regime lost the most active part of its working population. On August 13, 1961, the Berlin Wall was built, not to protect Communism against invasion but to stop that exodus. Cruel as it is, the Wall of shame proves the strength of anti-Communist feelings. The East Germans are forced to live under Communism. But they are not convinced. Freedom has the greater appeal.

FOREIGN-POLICY GOALS

German foreign policy must focus around three main aims: to keep peace; to secure freedom; and to bring about by peaceful means the reunification of the country. In the years between 1950 and 1955 a bitter fight took place over the question of what specific kind of foreign policy would link these three aims together. The majority under Chancellor Adenauer believed that a West German military contribution to NATO would give the West such miltary superiority that not only would peace and freedom be maintained where they existed but also the Soviet Union would be forced to yield in Germany and to open the way for reunification.

This concept failed. The Western military effort resulted in one great achievement: it stopped the Soviet advance in Europe and secured the freedom of Western Europe, with West Germany and West Berlin included.

But the NATO collective-defense system was not primarily designed to bring about reunification of Germany. It could only have served as a basis for negotiation. A strong alliance can never be blackmailed at the conference table. A purely military posture, however, especially in the atomic age, does not resolve political disputes. It has to be joined with a political effort.

The Social Democrats wanted to try for other security arrangements, based on *one* Germany instead of the partition of the country. This might have been possible in the early 1950's. It was not explored. But conditions have changed since that time. Therefore all the responsible groups in the German political system have to understand that the foreign-policy slogans of 1950 can no longer be applied in the same form in 1965.

After 1945 there was general agreement in Germany and outside that there should never be an armed Germany again. This consensus was understandable after the terrible experiences of two world wars. And it was also a result of the successful re-education which the German soul was exposed to by the Western Allies. The picture changed somewhat in 1948 when the Berlin blockade took place. It changed more when the Czechoslovakian coalition government fell and the Communists took power there, still more when the Korean War broke out. Then a good deal of discussion took place in the Western world about whether a German contribution to common defense was necessary. NATO had been founded in 1949 without Italy and the Germans. Looking backwards (not in anger but in confidence), it is fair to say that NATO has served its purpose: since its foundations were laid, there has been no more successful Communist aggression in Europe.

A debate on the possibility of German participation in NATO began in 1950. For many reasons, there was a good deal of sentiment in Germany and elsewhere against such participation. There were arguments for other alternatives, which were favored by many in the years from 1950 to 1955. Why? At that time the United States disposed of a monopoly in atomic weapons and strategic aircraft. The United States could hit every part of the Soviet Union without even ordering a blackout or a curfew at home. At that time the Russian fear of a German-American combination in the military field was greater and more plausible than it would be later. No effort was made to exploit that fear in a serious attempt at German reunification. If the more or less open invitations in the Soviet notes after 1952 had been taken advantage of, European security arrangements based on one Germany, instead of on military integration of the two parts of Germany in the framework of two opposite military alliances, might have been made. Time to explore this was available, for five years passed between the time the first discussions took place in 1950 and the time when the Federal Republic of Germany definitely entered NATO in 1955.

What were the alternatives? Some of them were not very realistic; others were more so. Neutrality, for example, could never be regarded as a serious possibility, because a neutral country must have the capacity to defend itself against every possible aggressor without foreign help. What gigantic armed forces a united Germany would have needed in that case to defend herself against possible Soviet aggression and even perhaps against American hostilities! Neutrality would have meant keeping all foreign powers at arm's length. We cannot assume that the Germans were ready or willing or able to support this, or that the other countries would have allowed the rearming of Germany in such a fantastic way. Imposing neutralism on an unarmed Germany was no solution either. Both the Russians and the Americans would have feared that overnight the power vacuum would have been filled by the other side. Moreover, unarmed neutrality would have created conditions of discrimination forever against one single nation in the whole world, leaving her defenseless, open to every form of aggression or blackmail.

Perhaps there was a chance for an exclusively European security arrangement involving several countries besides Germany with an agreed limitation of the armed forces of all participants under proper international inspection and with a guarantee by the great powers. It is impossible to know now whether such a European security system could have been established.

The possibility of reunifying Germany was not explored, and this gave the new German armed forces a very bad psychological start. Had the question been successfully explored, history would have taken a much healthier turn. A free united Germany with Berlin as capital would have contributed to a better solution of the political and security problems in Central Europe. Had the exploration ended without success, it would have been clear that neither the West nor the German govern-

ment were at fault but that Soviet posture led to the enforced solution to defend West Germany in the framework of the Western Alliance. This can be said without
bitterness. That part of history cannot be resurrected.

This train has left, because the political and strategic
situation has completely changed. The Soviet Union now
possesses a very wide scale of atomic weapons, and since
the orbiting of Sputnik and other events we know of the
precision and capacity of Soviet rocketry. All this points
to a kind of stalemate in the power relations in the world.
This gain in the strength of the Soviet Union had consequences for her policy toward Germany, reflected in
the ultimatum against Berlin in 1958 and in the attempt
to seal definitely the partition of the country by formal
international agreement. (The Soviets — I witnessed this
when I had a long talk with Premier Khrushchev in 1959
— lived in a kind of euphoria of power. This was somewhat dampened later by the Cuban experience and by
the disputes inside the Communist bloc.)

The security problem in Europe will remain part of
any future definite settlement of the German problem,
but the time is gone when European security could alone
be the key for the future of Germany. We have to regard
the problem in a larger context, including progress toward disarmament, measures of arms control, other East-
West relations, developments inside the Soviet bloc, the
Soviet conflict with China, the economic interests and
trade policy of the growing European Economic Community. East-West trade should be better organized than
it is now. The Soviet Union conducts its trade as *one*
importer and *one* exporter. The competition between

Western countries and Western firms is therefore a disadvantage to the West already in the purely commercial field. The Soviets use their economic power, limited as it might be, for political purposes. Why does the West not act in the same way? Even a complete embargo would not destroy Communism now that it has existed for half a century. But trade as an end in itself is giving away for nothing a political weapon. Long-range credits amount to development aid. Should this be given to a power like the Soviets without any political return? There are chances of a selective and better coordinated trade policy to bring political dividends. This in turn might create better conditions for a new approach to the German problem.

That is one of the reasons why Germany should take a more active and positive part in the Western efforts to reach arms-control agreements. So long as German soil is used as one of the sites of the arms race, partition will be all the harder to end. Progress toward disarmament will not automatically solve the German problem. The superpowers might agree to permanent partition. German foreign policy has to work skillfully in order not to disturb the disarmament negotiations but to present ideas that can help disarmament *and* the future of Germany at the same time. The German foreign service needs more resources to follow all the closely related problems of technology, geography, strategy, political interests, and psychology involved in these matters.

During the years of debate about rearmament in Germany, pacifist feelings were expressed in the nation and were widespread in the Social Democratic Party. This party in its basic program has never been a pacifist party as such. It has always stood for the defense of freedom against enemies inside the society or outside. Defense is necessary so long as no better international order has been created whereby national or allied defenses can be replaced by a kind of world order with the necessary amount of force to deter a possible breaker of the law. Unfortunately, it will take rather a long time to introduce into the relations among states the same amount of civilization that exists in relations among the citizens inside one state. We can only hope that the use of force by individual states against others will be replaced by respect for law and treaties, with the enforcement of laws and treaties through courts and international police if necessary.

The example of the German-French reconciliation will perhaps help to overcome the fears that Germany's eastern neighbors still feel as a result of historical experiences. This reconciliation genuinely involves the two nations, not only their governments. But in the general view of the German Parliament, this rapprochement should not be directed against others. Good relations between France and Germany are essential for the European Communities and for Western solidarity. There is no Europe without France, but no European security without the United States. Negotiations over the German problem can take place only with the Soviet Union, not with the puppet regime in the Soviet Zone of Germany. That regime wants nothing but the confirmation of partition, because in the event of a united Germany it would be fired by the electorate. For negotiations with the Soviets, a partner of equal size is required. Germany alone has not this stature. The Soviets try to isolate West Germany from the West. Then they could enforce their conditions. It is therefore vital for West Germany to keep strong ties with the West and to bar the Soviet attempts to isolate her. Whatever weakens Western solidarity is therefore detrimental to German interests. The friendship with France cannot induce Germany to support the present French military policy. Germany is for more integration, not for less. Admiration for De Gaulle's courage in liquidating colonialism and gratitude for his contribution to Franco-German friendship (which others started before him) must not lead to acceptance of his philosophy as a model for Germany or to approval of his stand against integration in Europe.

The Federal Republic of Germany wants a strong European Community with community institutions and parliamentary control. She wants Great Britain and others to have the opportunity to join, and she would like the free European neutrals to get fair treatment. She is in favor of a world-wide liberal trade policy (though this would create some difficulties for the present German government in regard to its somewhat protectionist farm policy). Germany wants a united Europe as an equal partner of the United States. This must be an organized community, not just a group of more or less sovereign nations.

And a sound German policy would call for more consultation in NATO. Much can be said for the wisdom of another policy in regard to China than that pursued by the U.S.A. over the last decade. But let us not act unilaterally as if there were no alliance at all!

Some people in Germany ask from time to time whether

there is not a contradiction between European or Western integration and the hope for German reunification. This is a real problem. Nobody should hide this. Nevertheless, there is a good case to be made against making European integration wait until German reunification is achieved. To seek unification that way would encourage the Soviet Union to refuse the reunification of Germany forever, because by that action they would forever stop progress in the field of European integration. In my view we should not be willing to pay that double price for nothing. We should patiently carry on the work of the Alliance and the Community and create better conditions for successful negotiations later. We are a defensive alliance.

The West has made it quite plain that there is no hope for the Communists to overrun Europe, and I am convinced that European integration has made it quite plain to them that they have no hope of profiting from our differences. The changes in the balance of political strength created by the European Community and by the strengthening of the Alliance may create new possibilities of approach to the German problem. This is a long-range prospect that requires discipline, patience, and courage. The West cannot force its solution of the problem on the Soviet Union, but we do not have to allow the Soviet Union to force her solution upon us. The loss of Berlin and the surrender of the other part of Germany forever to a Communist regime are not acceptable. In the meantime we can do certain things to ease the difficulties for human beings suffering behind the Wall, but only if we do so without jeopardizing a future solution which is also their future.

The question arises frequently as to whether the Germans indeed would still want to live in one state. The events at Christmas, 1963, gave a remarkably clear answer to that question. The meeting of more than four million Germans in the homes of East Berlin — more than one million living there, one million coming from West Berlin, two million from the Soviet Zone, and more than 60,000 from West Germany — proved that the Germans cannot be separated by barbed wire and the Wall, that they remain *one* nation and will continue to be one.

Chairman Ulbricht suffered a striking defeat in those days. He lost every control over this gigantic gathering. For the first time since 1945, traffic jams occurred on the broad streets of East Berlin, caused by the sudden invasion of West German cars. The inhuman procedure of making visitors wait all day and night before the passes were issued, the restriction to certain days and hours, with the obligation to be back in West Berlin before midnight, the admittance only through some carefully chosen gates in the Wall — these gave to the whole world the true picture of the free citizens of a country visiting their relatives in prison. Ulbricht tried to avoid a similar exposure in the future by asking for a political price that should change this demonstration of the will for unity into an act of recognizing partition. Neither the Senate of Berlin (the state government there) nor the federal government would pay that price, and they will not do so in the future.

The population of West Berlin knows that their existence in freedom gives hope to the Germans suffering from the imposed Communist regime. It is in the interest of the whole nation, the separated part included, that four-power responsibility for the whole of Berlin should remain in force and that the three Western powers continue to concern themselves with the freedom of West Berlin. Everybody knows also that West Berlin can survive in freedom only if the links with the Federal Republic of Germany, forged over fifteen years, are not loosened.* Without the participation of West Berlin in the currency system of the West German Deutsche Mark, its economy would collapse. West Berlin is therefore part of the economic system of the Federal Republic of Germany and enjoys considerable subsidies coming from there. But these links have more than economic importance. They are of extreme political and psychological value. They prove that a definite settlement of the German problem has not taken place and therefore that there is still hope for a better fate for the Germans on the other side of the Iron Curtain.

The physical presence of the Federal Republic of Germany in West Berlin is a necessity to protect the status of the Western powers in West Berlin, not an incursion against it. That status is derived from the four-power status for the whole of Berlin to which the three

* In this respect, the joint statement issued by France, Great Britain, and the United States after the Soviet Union concluded a "treaty of friendship" with the Soviet Zone of Germany in June 1964 was heartening. "The government of the Federal Republic of Germany is the only German Government freely and legitimately constituted," the three powers stated, "and therefore entitled to speak for the German people in international affairs." They affirmed that "West Berlin is not an 'independent political unit' " and that ties between Berlin and Bonn "are in no way inconsistent with the quadripartite status of the city and will be maintained in the future." *The Bulletin* (Bonn), vol. XII, no. 25 (June 30, 1964), p. 1.

Western powers justly stick. Only the presence of the Federal Republic of Germany in West Berlin, through the functioning of some officials and through meetings of the Bundestag and its committees, can maintain the equilibrium when all the administration of the Communist regime, the so-called "People's Chamber" included, is concentrated on the other side of the Wall. A resignation, a withdrawal of federal authorities from West Berlin would be an additional step in favor of the Ulbricht regime. It would shrink the four-power status to West Berlin alone, giving to the Soviets a right to interfere in West Berlin without corresponding possibilities for the Western powers in East Berlin.

Needless to say, in addition to the long-range political importance of Berlin, West Germany acknowledges the responsibility of caring for the interests of over two million Berliners who by their courageous fight on a besieged island have shown their dedication to freedom and democracy. It is interesting to know that the working-class quarters of Berlin, where before 1933 the Communist Party had its strongholds, have become the safest constituencies for the Social Democratic Party under the late Mayor Reuter and now Mayor Brandt. The SPD has won a majority of more than 60 per cent of the electorate in a "proletarian bastion." (See Table 2.) Such was the immunizing effect of a Communist regime compared to a democratic government under Social Democratic leadership in the same city! It is no wonder that the Berliners were as early as 1948 the first to accept the American troops in the name of protection more than occupation, even if Berlin is now the sole place in Ger-

Table 2. Postwar Voting in Berlin

A. Elections in West and East Berlin, 1946

Party	West Berlin		East Berlin		Totals West and East Berlin	
	Number of votes	Percentage of votes	Number of votes	Percentage of votes	Number of votes	Percentage of votes
SPD (Social Democrats)	674,209	51.7	341,400	43.6	1,015,609	48.7
CDU (Christian Democrats)	316,205	23.6	146,220	18.7	462,425	22.2
SED (Communists)	179,124	14.8	233,458	29.9	412,582	19.8
LDP (Liberal Democrats)	133,433	9.9	61,289	7.8	194,722	9.3
Totals	1,302,971	100.0	782,367	100.0	2,085,338	100.0

B. Elections in West Berlin, 1954, 1958, 1963

Party	Number of votes			Percentage of votes		
	1954	1958	1963	1954	1958	1963
SPD	684,906	850,127	962,197	44.6	52.6	61.9
CDU	467,117	609,097	448,459	30.4	37.7	28.8
FDP (Free Democrats)	197,204	61,119	123,382	12.8	3.8	7.9
DP (German Party — Conservatives)	75,321	53,912	...	4.9	3.3	...
SED	41,375	31,572	20,929	2.7	1.9	1.4
Splinter parties	69,970	10,681	...	4.6	0.7	...
Totals	1,535,893	1,616,508	1,554,967	100.0	100.0	100.0

Source: *Berliner Statistik,* published by the Senate of Berlin.

many where their legal position is still that of occupation.

As Berlin shows in a convincing way, the democratic forces must prove that the interests of the nation are safest in their hands. If they do not, then in the future others might bring up questions of unification and alliance in a dangerous manner. The polls in Germany show a growing public interest in the problem of reunification. Whereas in a poll in 1951 some 45 per cent of the respondents answered that building up the economy was the most important issue for Germany, only 21 per cent of a similar sample polled in 1963 placed economic questions first, and 31 per cent named reunification as the most important problem. Reunification is now the top issue, and this is especially true for the younger generation, for that generation which was born after Hitler came to power and which now constitutes nearly half the German population. The younger generation is aware of the past. But they ask why their generation should be punished permanently for what their fathers did. They do not deny German responsibility. They are on the whole a clear-headed generation, without myths, and they have no illusions about world powers agreeing to a German peace treaty out of pure benevolence.

Germany in her foreign policy is right to insist that boundaries should be fixed only in an open document at the conference table, not by de facto actions and tacit agreements. As long as no peace treaty has settled the subject, every German government will advocate the borders of 1937.

Several elements must be kept in mind in considering the specifics of reunification. First, there are no border problems in regard to Czechoslovakia. Second, Germany is not trying to play down the fact that Hitler started and lost World War II. Instead she is acutely aware that the consequences endure in the uncertain fate of more than 9 million expellees driven out from former parts of Germany. Third, Poland cannot base its policy on two contradictory assumptions: (a) that there should be two independent sovereign German states, but (b) that the state which in that case would not be a neighbor to Poland should be a prime figure in determining the boundaries of the other. If Poland wants a political declaration from the Bonn government on this problem, she should understand that she is discussing in fact the border of her future neighbor, a united Germany. Under these auspices, talks between West Germans and Poles are useful and could lead to a common proposal which could be presented to a future peace conference. Fourth, Poland should also realize that the Germans want to become as good neighbors to her as to France. She was the first victim of Hitler's aggression. The establishment of permanent governmental trade missions has taken place and will prepare the dialogue — let us hope a useful one.

I think that it is in Germany's interest to first agree at home on a consistent foreign policy, to defend that common stand in the Alliance, and through the Alliance to challenge our opponents in world politics. We regret that doubts about the course of German foreign policy are created again and again by disputes inside the government. Of course, the principles of foreign policy have to be open to discussion in a democratic state. But the other members of the Alliance deserve to know with what authority the chancellor and his foreign minister can truly commit the Federal Republic. Their standing is doubtful as long as the chairman of the Christian Democratic Party and the chairman of its Bavarian branch lead the internal opposition against the official foreign policy of West Germany.

What is being argued in Germany is whether the German influence on the French ally should be used to convince the French government of the necessity of European integration and of close cooperation with the United States or whether the French government should be encouraged to create under its leadership a separate European center of political and military decisions, independent from the United States. Is Western interdependence a necessity for common defense and survival? Or should the large European countries aspire to the role of independent world power again, with the implied danger of a revival of nationalism? This seems to be the other side of the same issue. For their part, the German Social Democrats regard Western interdependence as a fact and closer integration as vital. They will support the foreign policy of the government as long as it follows this line. This support will be given even if other trends strain the Alliance. The search for weaknesses to exploit in competing for power against the present government should not lead to artificial issues with dangerous consequences.

$\rightarrow\!\!\gg$ **4** $\ll\!\!\leftarrow$

The New Armed Forces

STRATEGIC ALLIANCE

AFTER A GREAT DEBATE in 1955, the Federal Republic
of Germany entered NATO and the Western European
Union (WEU). This latter group consists of Great Britain and the six countries of the European Communities
(Belgium, Luxemburg, the Netherlands, Italy, France,
and the Federal Republic of Germany). It had been
devised after the refusal of the plan for a European
Defense Community by the French national assembly
in 1954. Only within a framework which provided certain controls over the rearmament of Germany would
France accept the Federal Republic as a member of
NATO. So the original Brussels treaty, designed to protect five West European countries by very strong military
cooperation against a possible revival of German militarism, changed its original character by admitting Italy
and West Germany as members. This was the new WEU.

The assistance clause in the Western European Union
is stronger than that of NATO. It calls for automatic
assistance with all means, military force included. NATO
did not go so far and even now does not go so far. The

command structure of NATO, the assignment of forces to NATO in peacetime, the regular common exercises, and the steady elaboration of defense planning lead toward automatic assistance, but the treaty itself does not. The treaty leaves it up to every nation to decide by what means it will defend a friend in case of aggression. It could be a diplomatic action or a letter of condolence, but it could be the H bomb, too. With such a wide range of possibilities, the question of how NATO as such would take the political decision to go to war remains problematic.

WEU with its clause of automatic assistance is theoretically much more binding in this respect. But it has no command structure. This is left to NATO. The minimum force levels every member should provide, the requirements in number, equipment, location, and training are agreed upon in NATO. By contrast, WEU fixes the maximum level of the forces of its member states on the European continent and has created an inspection system to see that the limits are not exceeded. In WEU it has also been laid down that there must be no production of nuclear weapons in Germany. A special WEU arms-control agency is in existence in Paris, and perhaps the experience of this agency can serve in later arrangements for arms control on a wider scale. The precautions built into WEU were the result of understandable French fears about German rearmament. During the negotiations on the European Defense Community that failed in 1954, one could detect a certain French tendency, however, to ask for a German army stronger than the Soviet one but weaker than the French one, which was just a little bit difficult to achieve. To sum up, Western European Union was, in the beginning, a way of allowing German rearmament and at the same time controlling it.

WEU is confronted now with a new difficulty. The treaty prescribes that in case one of the members which has not renounced nuclear weapons starts production of such weapons in the future, then the council of the Western European Union will by a majority decision set limits to the stock, and the arms-control agency is supposed to see that these limits are respected. We have not the slightest indication that the French government will now come to the council and ask what stocks of nuclear arms should be fixed and how this can be controlled by WEU. Moreover, the minimum commitments underwritten in NATO for the force levels are far from being fulfilled except by the United States. Though the Federal Republic has made progress in this respect over the last years, some others have not. Neither the British nor the French contribution exactly corresponds to the commitments of the treaty. It is obvious that if there are international commitments, they should bind all, not merely some, of the partners.

German defense expenditures have been growing over the last years, as shown in Table 3. For the sake of comparison with other countries, we should not look into the defense budget alone. There are related budgets for Berlin, for the consequences of the last war – payments to widows, orphans, disabled veterans, and victims of Nazi persecution. I know quite well that these expenditures are necessary morally, that they are a consequence of the last war. The cost of making retribution for the

Table 3. Annual West German Defense Expenditures
(in German marks)

Year	German forces	Contribution to Allied forces	Combined
1955	1,601,557,600	10,070,267,300	11,671,824,900
1956	7,312,109,000	4,589,540,700	11,901,649,700
1957	7,801,400,000	2,145,874,700	9,947,274,700
1958	10,000,000,000	702,359,700	10,702,359,700
1959	10,994,088,800	777,641,100	11,771,729,900
1960	10,000,000,000	719,833,800	10,719,833,800
1961	11,185,200,000	552,626,700	11,737,826,700
1962	14,976,770,900	628,430,700	15,605,201,600
1963	18,360,000,000	466,956,900	18,826,956,900
1964	19,214,608,500	457,651,900	19,672,260,400

Source: Annual budgets.

criminal acts of the former German government cannot be counted as defense expenditures even though they are a burden on the gross national product. Germany cannot spend her money twice. The nation admits that it has to fulfill its commitments, but it is unfair to ask one country to carry a separate load of its own *and* to fill a gap that others leave. More cooperation inside the Alliance is desirable. The political balance inside the Alliance would be seriously shaken and an unfavorable political effect created if the military contribution of West Germany comes to overshadow that of all the other European allies.

The way in which every nation brings its contribution into existence is left to national decisions. NATO fixes the levels but not the methods of reaching them. In Germany we had a political fight over the introduction of conscription. There was a dispute about whether a professional army would not have been a better solution. In the long run, modern technology argues for a professional army where the soldier is kept well trained and well equipped in a highly mobile operational force made up of more or less permanent units. To train conscripts who soon leave the armed forces is very costly and does not give the proper return. But in a time of full employment, such as West Germany has now, it would be quite difficult to recruit armed forces on a long-term basis. Therefore at the moment and for the foreseeable future the manpower situation forces Germany to maintain conscription.

In her legislation the Federal Republic of Germany has introduced provisions for conscientious objectors. There are very few of these objectors. Subject to the approval of special committees, they are exempt if they are ready to render other services outside the armed forces for the community.

After the fight over conscription, the issue of nuclear weapons raised a strong debate. The majority in Parliament voted to equip the German armed forces "with modern weapons." The motion was phrased in just that sort of general language, without any qualification. However, from the Christian Democrat speeches during the debate a kind of understanding was reached that the government could be considered empowered to do anything short of the H bomb. Since the motion was passed in 1958, the Christian Democrat government fortunately has clarified its position, and the Social Democrats have modified their stand from the other end. There is now more explicit understanding and agreement. Christian Democrat officials made it quite plain that not only would no nuclear weapons be produced on German soil, as is laid down in the Paris agreements, but also that their government did not want unilateral German possession or powers of decision over nuclear weapons. They indicated a preference for integration of all nuclear weapons in the framework of NATO. They aimed at having a certain influence but not national competence. This is a far healthier position, which could lead to a certain participation in strategic planning.

The Social Democrats, for their part, came to see that the West ought not to give up nuclear weapons unilaterally as long as the Soviet Union not only maintains nuclear weapons but also disposes of an immense superiority in other weapons. Therefore the world-wide balance of power made a Western nuclear arsenal necessary. And in relation to the so-called tactical nuclear weapons on German soil, we must understand that even if they are not used, their presence gives a better chance for defense against conventional attack. The presence of these weapons makes it risky for a potential aggressor to concentrate his troops for a massive conventional attack, and therefore chances for conducting a successful non-nuclear defense are better.

If the concept of deterrence makes sense, it means that Western defense capabilities should deter aggression and therefore keep peace. To deter a concentration of hostile troops, Western troops with identical missions must have identical equipment. But tight control through the chain of command and by technical devices is necessary to ensure that no local commander, whether American or German, could change the character of warfare by deciding independently at the front to use nuclear warheads. This is one of the reasons for American custody over nuclear warheads assigned to means of delivery in European armed forces.

The West should not rely excessively on atomic weapons. Western defense must allow for alternatives other than surrender or suicide, because atomic warfare in any form would for the countries in the front line in Europe be tantamount to suicide. There must be safeguards against military hazards other than all-out nuclear war, too.

Where deterrence counts ultimately is not in our defense posture or our ideas but in the brain of a possible aggressor. Our deterrent is only credible if the aggressor is convinced that in case he attacks, it will be used. A threat to commit suicide is not very convincing, but the likelihood that hostilities can easily degenerate into suicide on both sides in case the attack cannot be stopped quickly is more credible. Therefore the West must be able to deter, to defend itself in case deterrence fails (only *this* capability will in fact deter), and to survive in case of defense. This means that the amount of force used in case of aggression must be proportionate to the threat: enough to defeat aggression but not so much as to uncontrollably wreak more destruction than is strictly required for fulfilling the defensive mission. The West must therefore dispose of a large spectrum of arms and a great variety of forces and cannot rely on atomic weapons alone. They are the last resort and not the automatic response to any kind of threat. A country which neglects its other forms of defense in favor of atomic weapons has no defense at all against the more likely forms of aggression.

The necessary Western defense posture cannot be created by each country separately. Only cooperation, an effective division of labor, and military integration can reach the aim. No single member-state of NATO, not even the United States, can afford to maintain all the necessary forces in kind and number. But all the common effort of the Alliance should serve to protect the security and the freedom of every single member state. This is the logic of the existing interdependence of the Western nations, created by geography, cultural ties, technology, and the cost of modern defense.

In that system, every country should take part in the over-all planning in such a way that it can be convinced that its needs are covered. Common planning, common decisions on the development of future weapon systems, on the size, equipment, and deployment of forces, are possible in peacetime. These decisions prefigure the ultimate decision to use atomic weapons. Participation in the decision-preparing process is therefore a real participation in decision making, even if, for reasons of speed, credibility, and expediency, that formal last decision will for a long while have to be reserved for the political leader of the strongest member, the president of the United States.

Some European members have been dissatisfied with their lack of influence on strategic decisions in the atomic field. As long as no better system has been found, the MLF (multilateral force) can be regarded as a good step in the right direction. It would bring more European cooperation to planning in this field, and by giving the members experience in handling nuclear weapons and a greater share of responsibility would advance their nuclear education. It is a paradox that countries possessing nuclear weapons are most careful in envisaging their use, while countries without a serious nuclear capability indulge in wild strategic concepts that promote an early and indiscriminate of these weapons. They obviously ignore the consequences of that kind of warfare for themselves, looking hypnotically at the assumed deterrent effect.

In the system of interdependence advocated here, as also in MLF as a possible first step (the second being a gradual transfer of ever more U.S. nuclear potential to that institution), the Federal Republic of Germany would not acquire nuclear weapons for herself or the power to launch nuclear warfare by her own decision. But she would be put on the same level as the other European partners. This, indeed, is essential. Discrimination against one single nation is bad policy. It has always been the seed for hostile nationalist feelings. We should never again build up the kind of national frustration which undermined the Weimar Republic. We should try to stop proliferation of nuclear weapons in general, but not develop a policy to withhold them from Germany alone.

If Europe wants a larger responsibility in military matters, she can win this by strengthening her unity and by making a greater effort toward real partnership for the United States. Equal partnership means also more responsibility in other than European affairs. Such a position cannot be reached by aspirations, but only by performance. Even if in the future Europe unites more closely and gains military strength, her defense effort should be integrated with that of the United States. Only then will an economic use of our resources be possible, an adequate defense posture attainable without financial and social ruin. A "go it alone" policy by Europe in the military field would weaken the West, aggravate the military risks in Europe, and as a natural consequence revive isolationism in the U.S. These ideas come fairly close to those which have been developed over recent years in the United States.

DEMOCRATIC SAFEGUARDS

In 1955, when I had to give an address at the Rhein-Ruhr Club to a more or less hostile audience composed mainly of industrialists, I explained the position of my political friends on the subject of the possible impact of armed forces on our internal affairs. I said that if Germany was to have armed forces, I had made up my mind long since that the generals would have to stand at attention for me and not I for them. An old gentleman, obviously a former officer, rose and said he would never do this. And my answer was: "It's good to hear this now, in time. Then there will be no trouble at all. There will be political leadership over the armed forces. Those, like you, who do not accept this principle, will not be taken into the army again." I think here you have in a nutshell the problem of democracy and militarism in Germany.

The spirit of the armed forces is at least as important as matériel and organization. The Social Democratic

Party insisted that if there were to be new German forces at all, they had to fit the framework of a democratic society. This was one of the lessons Germany had to learn from her past. There is an aphorism attributed to Mirabeau at the time of the French Revolution: that Prussia was not a state with an army but an army in possession of a state. This was not always an appropriate remark during the nineteenth century, but there was a certain tendency in that direction, and that tendency should never be allowed to reassert itself. In 1918, after the breakdown of the empire, the state was new but had inherited the old army. Although reduced in size, the army had its same structure, spirit, and generals, even its flags. In 1955, the opposite case was true. The state had existed since 1949 and created its army on a new plan. It was no continuation of Hitler's army.

The important new legislation by which the army was created included amendments to the constitution. Not only was all this drafted in cooperation with the Social Democratic opposition, but a good deal of the legislation was pushed through by that opposition with support from the other political parties against some conservative-minded minorities. The main point was to ensure political control, to vest leadership in the civil government. This is not identical with leadership of the military by civil servants. Both are part of an executive branch which itself is under control of Parliament. Civil servants should not run the armed forces, nor should the armed forces run the civil service. Neither arrangement is desirable, and therefore both parts of the executive need the leadership of the elected government and control by the elected Parliament. For that reason, the Federal Republic of Germany did not appoint an independent military high commander. And the president of the Federal Republic of Germany could not be placed at the top of the military hierarchy, because the president is not responsible to Parliament at all. He has no executive function. Therefore the real position of commander of the armed forces in peacetime was given to the minister of defense as a member of the cabinet, and in wartime to the chancellor, in order to concentrate power at such a time when it is necessary. This is more or less theoretical, because in wartime NATO will hold command. This will be no German problem at all. But provision had to be made for contingencies not covered by a treaty. Germany hopes that NATO will be continued, but this is not certain. The constitution cannot follow the lines of international agreements alone.

Control of the armed forces by Parliament is channeled through a powerful committee that is specifically named in the constitution and cannot be created or disbanded at will by a parliamentary majority. It is required by the constitution, and it has the power of investigation, similar to the investigative powers of the American Senate committees, which is rather unusual in terms of the European tradition. Furthermore, there is firm budget control. Of course a fuller and more exact specification of the military budget is given in committees of Parliament than in the printed budget. Such rules prevail in every country for reasons of protection of military secrets, but the whole budget with all the significant details is subject to Bundestag approval.

A Scandinavian institution has been taken over with great success — the special commissioner of Parliament for the armed forces. He has the right to inspect everything, to look into every file, to visit the troops, to demand information. He reports back to Parliament and back to the executive, and he can make proposals. He cannot give orders, because then he would be a kind of counter-minister, but his power of inspection and exposure is formidable. To propose certain settlements and certain legislation is in his powers, and the annual and special reports of this commissioner have already gained a certain importance for influencing the spirit of the German armed forces and for leading to reforms if necessary. Any member of the armed forces may complain to him directly without being subject to disciplinary action.*

The man who until recently was Armed Forces Commissioner had earlier been a member of Parliament for the Christian Democratic Party, but he was elected unanimously. He enjoyed the confidence of the House. His good contacts with the SPD group, where he spoke as to other groups, were not heartily welcomed by all his former political friends. When he gave — in an illustrated weekly paper — a more dramatic version of his findings

* The Armed Forces Commissioner is elected by a majority of the Bundestag in secret balloting. He reports to the president of the Bundestag during his five-year term of office, from which he may be expelled or to which he may be re-elected by a majority vote of the Bundestag. Any German at least thirty-five years of age who has the right to vote for the Bundestag and who has served one or more years in the German armed forces may be nominated. The Armed Forces Commissioner may not practice any paid trade or profession, participate in the management of any commercial enterprise, or belong to any governmental body, in either the federation or the states, during his term of office.

than in his official report, he came under heavy fire. But he deserves credit for opening a fundamental debate on some of the educational problems of the armed forces and on their own stand in a democratic society. This debate has taken such a turn that his retirement, for reasons of poor health following an accident, will not end in a weakening of the institution of the Armed Forces Commissioner, but on the contrary will ensure great attention to the work of that official and to its effects on the armed forces.

The commissioner serves as a kind of watchdog, not a watchdog committee but just one inspector with a small staff of civil servants. His job is to see that principles of modern leadership, of civil rights, and of human dignity are respected in the armed forces. For example, there must be a clear-cut line between the drill which is obviously necessary in every army to prepare men for combat and unnecessary mistreatment which runs counter to human dignity. This line can be drawn only by experience and not by theory.

A screening committee supervises the reappointment of staff officers. Its members, chosen for the great respect they enjoy in public life, are elected by, but do not belong to, the Bundestag. Unfortunately this committee has only the task of screening reactivated staff officers. It cannot intervene for new promotions inside the armed forces.

The legislation of the Bundestag in matters concerning the armed forces always holds a very great interest for the public. The constitution says that the rules of international law must be recognized in German law.

Therefore military orders have to be maintained in the framework of international law. Everything having to do with the armed forces has been brought under inspection of the minister and of Parliament. Of course, sometimes unfortunate events occur. Cases of military malfeasance can be found in Germany as in every nation, but such cases are no longer hidden as they were in the German past. Military affairs are given an airing in the press, sometimes to the detriment of the circles immediately concerned, but this is healthy, because public debate can then create better conditions and lead to corrections. West Germany does not segregate the armed forces from the normal life of the nation as in the past. Soldiers have the right to vote. They can even be candidates for the Bundestag, although they must resign from the service at the time. Soldiers on active duty cannot sit in Parliament, but they can vote, and therefore it is normal for them to develop a political stand of their own.

A new danger should be mentioned, and that is the one of the army's identifying itself with one party alone, with the party in power. This danger is always present and calls for special vigilance. It will create some problems in the future too. The Social Democrats had hard debates on these problems. They stand for a relation of mutual confidence between the armed forces and all the democratic forces in the country. But the opposition had also to show the virtue of its function, the virtue of democratic vigilance in regard to every action of the executive, including the armed forces.

Historical resentments had to be overcome on both sides, in political life and in the armed forces. Many

Social Democrats regarded the armed forces and every professional soldier as a threat to democracy and world peace. And many professional soldiers, especially career officers, regarded the Social Democratic Party as unreliable and more linked to internationalist and pacifist doctrine than to the necessity of defending the national community and its freedom. The split between the armed forces and the labor movement was one of the most important reasons for the weakness of the Weimar Republic. To create a better climate was necessary. With that, a new chapter in the history of the country opened. The SPD cooperated in shaping the constitutional and legislative articles pertaining to the military and appealed to party sympathizers and members to join the armed forces, even to consider career service if they had the necessary qualifications. It was unfair to complain of one-sided social and political composition in the armed forces if one great party withheld its own followers from them. If the armed forces were not to be isolated, then also the opposition party had to respect them and to participate. The SPD tried to introduce a regular intellectual intercourse between soldiers and all parts of our public life. Its Bundestag members often appear in the barracks, not for campaigning but in the interest of a better mutual understanding.

Some of the Christian Democratic government leaders did not like these activities. They wanted the opposition to be looked upon as having no understanding of the necessities of defense and of armed forces at all. By this kind of reasoning the armed forces, with more than 400,000 members and their families and the civilian personnel, could have become a kind of stronghold in the psychological warfare for keeping power at the next election against the opposition. This was and is still a temptation for the party in power. But these shortsighted views did not prevail. They are still held in some quarters, but there is now a somewhat better understanding that the armed forces need the support of the whole nation, not of one party alone. Examples prove that the members of the armed forces vote as other individuals and groups of our society do. A changing trend in the pattern of votes does not pass them by.

This is not simply the consequence of what the Social Democrats have done and of a better understanding of the problem by government and army leaders. It also reflects a change in the social composition of the armed forces. Our modern army is a highly technical outfit. There are no more second sons of feudal landowners as officers; the old names are still there, but the properties are lost somewhere in the East. Other economic and social developments have diminished the prestige of these old names. Those who bear them have become state employees or officials instead of landowners. Of course it is important to remain wary of special privileges in certain positions, but an old danger has passed with the old social structure. No more do the second sons of farmers in East Prussia comprise the noncommissioned-officer class. The East Prussian territories are not part of the Federal Republic of Germany, and most farmers coming as refugees to the free part of the country are integrated in an industrial society. Moreover, the professional soldiers who joined the German armed forces after

1955 had broadened their background beyond their World War II military experience. They brought with them their experience from all kinds of jobs in civilian life for more than ten years. This was quite new in Germany. The armed forces gained by that additional experience of their first cadre and did not take over an unbroken tradition of the past. Some people may long for the past, but their influence is offset by leaders who decided courageously that commemoration of the plot against Hitler on the 20th of July, 1944, should be made a formal part of the tradition of the new armed forces. Resistance for freedom is acknowledged to be better than blind obedience to crime and foolishness.

On the fifteenth anniversary of the 20th of July, for example, General Adolf Heusinger, Inspector-General of the Bundeswehr, issued a proclamation in which he said:

The deed of the 20th of July, 1944 — an act against injustice and oppression — is an auspicious break in Germany's most dismal period of history. Though confronted with the fatal probability that their action might fail, freedom-loving men of all strata of society — amongst whom soldiers stood in the front line — decided to overthrow the tyrant. . . .

We, the soldiers of the Bundeswehr, bow our heads in respect for those men whose conscience was evoked by their perception of the situation. Those men are the most distinguished witnesses against a collective responsibility of the German people. Their attitude and their spirit are exemplary to us.

The battle for the proper functioning of armed forces within a democratic framework will have to be repeated again and again, as sometimes the Civil War in the United States seems to be repeated again and again and reappears in different forms. The prospect for the spirit of the German armed forces now, however, is better than in the past, even with the limitations mentioned, because modern technology requires other qualities of men. A modern army needs engineers, skilled workers, men with scientific background. They are indispensable, and for that reason the new German armed forces are now a more representative cross-section of the society than in the past. This is another help to avoid a new gap between soldier and worker.

At present the Bundeswehr suffers from a shortage of officers and of noncommissioned officers. The shortage results from full employment in the civilian economy and from the uncertain standing of the armed forces in public opinion. There are always ups and downs in the public attitude toward the armed forces. Sometimes public opinion regards army discipline as too strict, sometimes as too weak. We had those events at Nagold where some noncommissioned officers, obviously with the approval of the officers, went too far in mistreating their men. They appeared before a court and have been sentenced. The newspapers report similar events in other armed forces of the world. This is not a German specialty, and some troops who call themselves "elite" are sometimes very proud of the rough treatment they get when they are young. This applies especially to paratroopers and marines in certain countries.

Hanson Baldwin writing in the *New York Times* of May 6, 1964, argues that West Germany has gone too far in elaborating all the safeguards mentioned above. He believes that military efficiency has suffered from this trend. I do not share this view. All these measures have created a better psychological climate in the nation for the armed forces. This is very important for their fighting value. Foreign correspondents should not too easily accept the opinions of those who wish to come back to past traditions. There might have been exaggerations in the new course. But they are not the rule. If the quality of the German forces still has not achieved the high standard aimed at, a number of technical reasons can be given. The spirit of "modern leadership" is not to blame. Far more relevant are the speed with which the forces were raised, the lack of officers and noncommissioned officers, supply problems, and the failure to create a uniform NATO logistics system.

Other points of relevance are the psychological problem of rearmament in a divided country and the psychological problem of the possibility of nuclear warfare in a country which would be annihilated during the very first moments. These problems explain an additional set of psychological difficulties which affect the shaping of the Bundeswehr. Our young people — and this is a psychological change — are not keen on serving as draftees. Formerly in Germany it was assumed that a man was not a man until he had served in the army. Now Germany is coming back to the normal psychological reactions of younger generations everywhere, who understand the necessity of service but do not believe that it is an obvious requirement for proving virility.

As for the effects of raising armed forces within the framework of the Alliance, they are in general healthy. The integration in NATO makes it quite clear that there is no possible isolated national defense. Germany could not go it alone. No risk of a German military adventure exists. The cooperation and joint staffs, the frequent contacts between men and officers of different countries, the learning of languages, the exchange of whole units, the training in other countries (West Germany has units in Great Britain and France, and some are trained in the United States) — these make for solidarity. Practice ranges in the Mediterranean are used by the German air force. And many forces from other countries are in Germany. More than 200,000 American soldiers are serving in Germany. This network leads to a good deal of understanding among young people just at an age when they are really impressed by their surroundings. I hope for more integration in logistics, because this would make it even more obvious that no national warfare is possible, but only an integrated defense against a possible aggression.

One remarkable development which deserves proper attention in all democratic countries is the influence of the "trade union of soldiers" — an international military interest group which is not quite in the spirit I like to see in the armed forces. There are no bad intentions. The difficult mission of defense and the special professional experience and interest lead the soldiers of all armed forces in the West to make agreements and then to hide them behind the screen of military secrecy. If, for example, NATO is quoted in Germany as making recommendations or setting requirements, we should always ask whether this is really NATO or whether it is only part of a military staff which has induced other NATO people to raise a cry for what they could not get at home. We must be sure that the military cooperation which is necessary is properly brought under civilian control in the international sphere too, that soldiers do not use the shield of secrecy against their own governments or parliaments.

If, for example, we are discussing emergency measures in Germany, we may be told that NATO would have this or that requirement. It is often far from certain that this really stems from the governments of the Western allies. Some "requirements" may come from an international military staff who has been advised by German military people what powers they want. Germany does not want to be duped into pro-military legislation, even if there are more troops on German soil. Of course, in this field as in other security areas, experienced military people should give proper advice. That is necessary and unavoidable. But these consultants cannot make the ultimate decision, which is a political decision and must be taken by the executive and by the legislature in their respective fields.

No military machinery can work unless orders are executed. I know that. But even those orders have to respect law, and the execution of orders has to start on top. The military commanders get orders from the civilian authority and not the other way round. I think that all this has set the stage for a certain amount of civic education through the army. Can the new federal army work in that field too? There is always more to be done in the way of inculcating democracy.

ATTITUDES AND VALUES

We must remember that many German parents do not wish to appear as fools before their children, and therefore they keep silent about the period between 1933 and

1945. Since this same reticence is found among the older generation of school teachers (although the younger ones are forthright), civic education of the younger generation still poses a difficult problem for Germany. Might the armed forces step in and take over the job of democratic training? I have my doubts. What the family, the school, the job, the union, the church, and all the rest of our society have not brought about, the armed forces, in the short time they have the soldiers with them, cannot do. They can add something, but others must have planted the roots. The Bundeswehr is not the school of the nation. This would be a misconception. Civic education during military training is possible only in a very limited way.

Civic education should give to the young citizen a true conception of his rights and duties in a democratic society. This cannot be achieved by learning the text of the constitution and of other laws. There are people who know these texts by heart and nevertheless behave as cowards without civil courage, just as there are others who know the whole Bible without living up to it. What counts is the dedication to the values written down in these texts, the personal engagement. The democratic virtues can be developed only in a democratic framework. Democracy works by discussion and vote, but the armed forces must insist on order and obedience. There is no democratic army; there is only an army in a democratic society. The armed forces should faithfully serve democratic governments and show respect for national and international law. Article 8 of the so-called Soldiers Act of 1956 in fact states: "It is the duty of a soldier to acknowledge the liberal democratic order within the meaning of the constitution and to uphold it by his general conduct." They should shape military procedures as far as possible along democratic lines. Article 29 of the Soldiers Act, for example, makes it mandatory to give a soldier a hearing before factual statements unfavorable to him are entered in his personal file — and "his comments must be included." Article 35 provides for the election by secret ballot of spokesmen for the various ranks within the various units, and these spokesmen may submit proposals on welfare matters to commanders. But training in democracy must take place elsewhere than in the armed forces.

This is the place to say a word on the national spirit of the Bundeswehr. Are they wholeheartedly NATO troops, or are they still at every turn German armed forces, and how do they envisage the future of their own nation? Of course they are German. But they know quite well that there is no German defense outside the framework of the Alliance and outside the European Community, and so a highly developed community spirit is part of the framework of the German armed forces.

Through this discussion of our armed forces and of some aspects of the spirit of the generation now entering our armed forces, I come to certain conclusions. Armed forces pose problems for every form of society. We in Germany, among my friends and party, had to learn how to handle armed forces. If we had not learned this, the forces would handle us. Nobody can predict the future precisely. This is fortunate, for life would be boring if there were no curiosity unsatisfied. But even without knowing what the future will bring, I dare say that the armed forces of the Federal Republic of Germany, integrated as they are in NATO and the European Community, are now in keeping with a democratic society and are under proper control of a civil government and a freely elected parliament.

I do not want to give the impression of lighthearted optimism. We know the problems, and we have to remain vigilant, but after all we have lived through, it may be excusable to dwell on improvements that have been made. Proof will come if our armed forces stand loyally under a new administration when a democratic change in government takes place. I am convinced that already the present precautions and legislation and screening and social composition give us the right to look forward with confidence to that possibility. Our armed forces will prove themselves. As a leader of the opposition, I might add, I should be very glad if they got that chance soon.

5

The Contribution of the SPD

THE SOCIAL DEMOCRATIC PARTY is Germany's oldest one. In 1963 it passed its hundredth birthday. This is not quite so hoary as it looks at first glance, however. The competing Christian Democratic Party which is now in power has re-elected a chairman who himself alone has nearly reached that age. That is former Chancellor Adenauer. The Social Democrats as the oldest party reflect the history of the nation over the past century, with the glory and misery, with the accomplishments and shame, with ups and downs. The SPD has always tried to safeguard democracy, and it achieved many results, but often it was defeated. I feel we must always be on the search for the reasons behind those defeats, and one has to look for these reasons inside the party as well as in external causes.

The Social Democratic Party again manifests a youthful, vital spirit. It is now stronger in Germany than ever before. Polls taken in the spring of 1964 showed that it was favored by 43 per cent of the electorate. This is a new record. In the elections of 1961, it had 38 per cent of the votes, which gave it 40 per cent of the seats in the Bundestag, and it achieved this without its original strongholds of support. Traditionally the party was never strong in that part of Germany which is now the Federal Republic. Its original strongholds are now under Communist domination. Saxony and Thuringen should be mentioned, as well as the industrialized former Prussian province of Saxony with Halle, Magdeburg, Merseburg (chemical industries), and Bitterfeld (lignite). The entire city of Berlin, once a center of SPD strength, no longer figures in elections, because East Berlin is cut off by the Wall and West Berlin sends members to the federal Parliament only by delegation from the state parliament. I was born in East Berlin, and I know what the working-class quarters of Berlin have meant for the SPD. Therefore one can safely say that the new strength in the free part of the country shows specifically the progress the Social Democrats have made over the last decade. In the time of the Weimar Republic the party polled on the average 25 per cent of the votes, not more. Because of the great splitting up in the other parties, for a certain number of years the Social Democrats were relatively the strongest party, but they never could run the country alone. In the fourteen years after 1918 in the Weimar Republic, they were partners in coalition governments only for five and one half years. For comparison the Catholic Center party was during all that time a partner in coalition, sometimes with the SPD, sometimes with others, until Hitler came to power.

UP FROM MARXISM

The SPD reformulated its political philosophy in basic manifestoes once in each generation. These successive documents give a clear picture of the trend of events in a modern society. After the rebuilding of the party following the twelve years of persecution under Bismarck's antisocialist law from 1878 to 1890, the important basic program of Erfurt was adopted by a party convention in 1891. It was strongly influenced by Marxist doctrine and showed a rather revolutionary spirit. Some thirty-four years later, in 1925, the convention at Heidelberg adopted a new program. After World War I and the breakdown of monarchy, after SPD cooperation in the central government and political control over a number of state governments and cities, that program of Heidelberg tried to adjust the party to the new situation. The task was now to influence the state and to bring about more democratic and social reforms instead of a revolutionary fight against state and society. All practical proposals in the program were shaped on that line, but the theoretical introductory chapters were still largely influenced by the Marxist school. Once again thirty-four years later, after another war, after another persecution of a far more dangerous and ruthless kind, after another political, economic and social rebuilding, the party adopted in 1959 at the special convention of Bad Godesberg, after a long careful debate in the rank and file, the latest basic program, serving as signpost for the policy and the public relations of the party.

Strongly Marxist in theory at the beginning, the party was in practice more flexible. This was a contradiction which surely did not add to credibility. It was a weakness compounded by dispute about various elements of Marxism itself. Ferdinand Lassalle, one of the founders in 1863, started with the doctrine that it was necessary to win the state, to make out of the state an instrument for shaping policy. Marx had the opposite theory that it was necessary to destroy the state and to rebuild on the ruins of the existing society a new order, and he had also the theory that in the future the state would disappear. (It would be tempting to investigate how far Lenin has really taken over Marxist ideas and how far his personal contribution was in fact a deterioration of Marxist philosophy. But this can be left open here because it is irrelevant to the purpose of this book. Nevertheless, it is interesting to note that in the Soviet Union, claiming to be the legitimate heir to Marxism, the state is far from disappearing and by the nationalization of all the means of production exercises a tighter control over the citizen and the whole society than any state in Marx's lifetime had.)

In founding their party, the Social Democrats envisaged opposition not only against the government but also against the existing state organization in general. But this was only part of the party's position. There was more in it. It was a natural uproar, a natural opposition against the exploitation and terrible conditions of life in the time of early capitalism. It was a protest against the denial of civil rights to the working man, who in most parts of Germany had not even the right to vote.

One of the early slogans of the party, put into a song the party sang in those years, was: free elections are the flag with which we win. This is a sign of the deep-rooted democratic tradition of the party. It sought power not through revolution or force but by persuasion and election. This fight for the right freely to elect a parliament, and through the parliament the government, is still of burning importance in Germany. It is not a closed chapter. In East Germany this human right is refused. In all Germany the right was refused to the nation between 1933 and 1945 by the Nazi dictatorship. This story of the fight for free elections by the Social Democrats over all their existence explains why they are so fiercely opposed to the Communist regime in the other part of Germany. They are proud to continue an old fight for democracy.

When the party was created, it was not an isolated phenomenon. There was quite a surrounding of sympathizing organizations in other fields of society — a kind of self-defense of the labor population and small artisans against the growing forces of big business and of the surviving feudal institutions in Germany. Therefore the trade-union movement was very close to the Social Democratic Party, as was the cooperative movement, especially in the field of consumer cooperatives. They were all created around that period one hundred years ago.

In 1891, when the manifesto of Erfurt was drafted, the Catholic church dealt with similar social problems in a famous document, the encyclical *Rerum novarum*, addressed to the new social conditions created by industrialism. Thus the organizing of the SPD was only one of many signs of change in Europe at the time. The SPD was fiercely resisted by the state, however, and — I must add — the Protestant church. Imperial and Protestant authorities defended with all possible means the existing social set-up, and from their acts stems a good deal of the antagonism and contradiction between the churches and the Social Democratic movement in Germany. As has already been mentioned, between 1878 and 1890, the party suffered the first period of legal persecution. It was outlawed by the antisocialist law of the Bismarck government, but when the law was repealed, the party came back stronger than before.

Yet, while fighting the whole social order of that time, the German Social Democratic Party always took a stand against foreign domination. If we read the speeches of the party's leaders in the Reichstag of those years, mainly of its chairman August Bebel, we find that they were always in favor of the defense of the nation against foreign aggression. What they fought for was a fair distribution of the cost of that defense, and what they fought against was the misuse of military power, the militarism of those days.

What they would not stand for was expressing unjustified nationalistic aspirations at the expense of other countries by military force. The few Social Democratic members of the first Bismarck parliament had supported the war of 1870 against Napoleon III as long as it could be regarded as a defense against provocation and foreign pressure. But after the fall of monarchy in France, the Social Democrats refused to continue a war against the newly born French republic, and they advocated a peaceful reconciliation without the seizure of French territory. This was — looking backward from the history of World War I — a very farsighted view, unfortunately not shared by the nation. On the contrary, this stand taken by the party led to prosecution of its leaders.

The SPD supported the defense of the nation in World

War I so long as the defensive purpose was credible. But later during the war, it tried to start a move for a peace without annexations, which was taken up by Parliament but had no consequences. A minority had left the party and formed an Independent Social Democratic Party, refusing to support the war effort and basing its policy on a more revolutionary doctrine. In November 1918, that party formed together with the majority Social Democrats the provisional German government, the Council of the People's Commissioners. The old party fought hard against the attempt to introduce a Soviet system in Germany and enforced the decision for holding free elections for a constituent national assembly in 1919. But only through a civil war against the left extremists could this decision be applied. A large group of the Independent Social Democrats under the leadership of the very popular Karl Liebknecht and Rosa Luxemburg had formed the Spartacus Association which later became the Communist Party of Germany (KPD). In January 1919 these two leaders were assassinated by troops fighting for the provisional government. This murder, which was never impartially investigated, gave to the Communists precious martyrs and was partly responsible for the special bitterness of the political fights after 1918. Even some loyal Social Democrats held reservations about the new republic as the result of this violence and the split on the left.

In 1922, the remainder of the Independent Social Democratic Party, after having lost a great part of their followers to the Communist Party, merged with the old party. This reunified SPD in 1925 at Heidelberg adopted the new basic program. That program maintained a Marxist vocabulary. It tried to explain in a somewhat doctrinaire way the whole history of mankind. The practice of the party, however, was that of reform, of settling down in the state organization, taking part in shaping the policy of the national government, of provincial governments, and of some cities where the party had come to power. That program said "yes" to the democratic republic, but not a wholehearted "yes." There was some feeling that this democratic republic should be regarded only as a transitional period to be left behind in the development of socialism.

Here again we must look to another interesting document coming from the Catholic church. In 1931 appeared the encyclical *Quadragesimo anno*, supplanting the encyclical *Rerum novarum* from forty years earlier. It was the time of mass unemployment. The new encyclical preached a new social order to overcome the difficulties of capitalism in the 1930's. It preached a kind of corporation state. This did not correspond to the ideas of the Social Democrats, but nevertheless it was something else than the existing pattern of society in the early 1930's. Perhaps Austria was a kind of experiment along these lines, beginning in 1934 and ending unhappily in 1938.

REJOINING THE NATION

Having spoken so much of certain parallel developments in the Catholic church and the Social Democratic Party, I must add here that the World War II partition of the country has changed the religious composition of Germany. Before partition Germany was two-thirds

Protestant and one-third Catholic, and now in the Federal Republic we are about equal between the two major religions. This has political consequences, especially because the Catholic church became the supporter of a political party, which normally should not be regarded as the proper function of a church in a democratic society. The Protestant church, which fought against the Social Democrats before 1914 and to a lesser degree under the Weimar Republic, now has taken a neutral stand. It is one of the most important events in the last five years that there are signs that the Catholic church is fortunately trying to disengage from direct participation in the party struggle. Many German Catholics are on the way to recognizing that a Christian citizen must have the possibility of a choice between different political parties in order to maintain the freedom of a society and in order not to arrive at a hidden one-party system. If all Christians had to unite in one party, there would not be much left for another party. A growing proportion of Catholics voted Social Democrat in recent years, especially in the former strongholds of their opponents. In Bavaria, for example, with one exception — the city of Würzburg — there is no city with more than 100,000 inhabitants which is not now governed by a Social Democrat mayor. In the Saar area, with a population more than 90 per cent Catholic, the SPD has become the strongest party, as it did in all of the large cities in the Ruhr basin at the last municipal elections in 1964.

There is also a good deal of thought in the Catholic church about the danger of taking responsibility for mistakes committed by a party, because this would be the

consequence if church and party were too closely identified. I found during my visit to Rome in March 1964 that
there was a good deal of intellectual movement in the
Catholic church in preparation for the next session of the
Ecumenical Council in September of that year. A certain
predisposition toward an open society is apparent in
some of the encyclicals of the late Pope John XXIII and
shows itself in the speeches which Pope Paul VI delivered
during his trip to Palestine. I think the most important
factor is that even tolerance is no longer regarded as
sufficient to explain the relations among different
churches, religious beliefs, convictions, and political parties in our mobile and open society. We have to replace
the word "tolerance" with "freedom." Tolerance means
that a majority merely allows a minority to subsist and
barely conceals its contempt. Freedom means that a
majority of those who are convinced that their faith is
alone the real one must respect the convictions of others.
I think this change of attitude will have consequences
not only for Germany but for all those countries in
Europe where in the past the Catholic church has directly intervened in favor of one political party. Such a
self-limitation of the church is not at all detrimental to
its right to take a stand publicly on matters regarding
our public life in sharpening the conscience of the citizens and their leaders.

This freer interpretation of tolerance, on which there
is now general agreement in the German Social Democratic Party since the adoption of the *Basic Programme*
at Bad Godesberg in 1959, is linked to other important
features in that document. That the militant, rigid Marx-

ist ideology has given way to a more open view of society is evident in the following passage from page 5 of the official English translation of the *Basic Programme*, which was published in several languages by the SPD:

Democratic Socialism, which in Europe is rooted in Christian ethics, humanism, and classical philosophy, does not proclaim ultimate truths — not because of any lack of understanding for or indifference to philosophical or religious truths, but out of respect for the individual's choice in these matters of conscience in which neither the state nor any political party should be allowed to interfere.

A party is no longer regarded as a church or as a counter-church. It is not a school of philosophers. It does not feel obliged to explain the history of mankind. This has to be left to the universities and individual thinkers and searchers. A party has to develop a concept of what a community should do, a concept based on values we share, and I think a high priority has to be given to our common notion of human dignity as well as to the notion of the freedom of a human being and of the freedom of the nation, limited only by the freedom of other human beings and other nations. Recognizing the necessities of community life and community organization, the party strives for the proper ordering of the unavoidable tension between freedom and society. We have also to create the material conditions which liberate human life from misery and hunger, from oppression and fear. (As I say this, a recent European maxim occurs to me: capitalism is the exploitation of man by man, and in communism it goes just the other way round.) The Bad Godesberg program brought a new line of understanding in the relation between political parties and churches in a democratic society. Their functions are different. They owe each other mutual understanding and respect, knowing also that the same people are active in both groups. They are not identical circles, but they overlap to a large extent.

The SPD's *Basic Programme* does not attempt to set the party against the state. "The Social Democratic Party of Germany lives and works in the whole of Germany" (p. 6). Nor does it try to hold the party aloof from everyday politics. The SPD "aims to win the support of the majority of the people by competing under equal conditions with other political parties" (p. 7). One of the weaknesses of the party in the Weimar Republic undoubtedly was that it did not understand political power as well as the opponents of the Weimar Republic — the extremists on both sides. Power in itself is neither good nor bad. What counts is how the competition for power is carried on, in what spirit power is used, and how power is kept in bounds by the electorate. That is the essence. It is crucial to carry on the struggle for power in a democratic way, not to misuse for the perpetuation of party dominance the power which has been delegated by the electorate, and to regard the team in power as a trustee who must go back to the electorate in order to be confirmed or replaced by another. One must understand also that power is necessary to execute one's political ideas. Ideas without power cannot change the situation, neither in the social nor in the economic field. This real sense of the necessity of power — in a nation as well as in a party — is rather a new experience among some

German progressive groups, and it gives the Federal Republic greater stability than the Weimar Republic had.

From that sense of power flows also a clear "yes" to the necessity of defense, against enemies of democratic freedom inside and out. Since the problems of defense have already been dealt with in Chapter 4, the point merely needs to be affirmed here in principle.

A hard fight took place in the party before its modern position with respect to economic life was fixed. The German Social Democrats have learned the hard way that nationalization is not the way to cure all the evils of our time. If there is but one employer, Mr. State, who is also in command of the police, then there is no freedom for the citizen and no freedom for labor and its unions. The *Basic Programme* declares (p. 10):

Free choice of consumer goods and services, free choice of working place, freedom for employers to exercise initiative as well as free competition are essential conditions of a Social Democratic economic policy. The autonomy of trade unions and employers' associations in collective bargaining is an important feature of a free society. Totalitarian control of the economy destroys freedom. The Social Democratic Party therefore favours a free market wherever free competition really exists. Where a market is dominated by individuals or groups, however, all manner of steps must be taken to protect freedom in the economic sphere. As much competition as possible — as much planning as necessary.

The SPD is in favor of competition between different forms of property. Individual property, public property, and cooperative property — each has its place in a modern framework. There should be no dogmatic stand on that. The state should not go into that field of economy where private business better serves the needs of the market, to adjust to its changes and to rationalize production and distribution of goods under the pressure of competition. But in some specific fields, where a huge investment is necessary, where private business cannot be expected to take certain risks, and where serious security interests are also involved, a tighter public control or public ownership might be necessary. Such is the case with atomic-energy facilities in most Western countries, at least as regards the production of fissionable material. The various and flexible forms of public and mixed property in the production and distribution of electrical power have been one of the essential bases for the speedy expansion of the economy in Germany after World War II. Similar arrangements are valid for such public utilities as water supply or public transport in the large cities.

In some fields of activity, a public share in an important producer can serve to maintain sharp competition in favor of the consumer. Such public participation, if competition is fair and not falsified by artificial subventions (such as fiscal ones), can in certain cases protect competition in a more efficient way than a legal procedure would do, although public shareholding in limited cases does not replace the need for general legislation in that field.

Modern technology and modern economic and social development pose many problems. We must protect competition from being destroyed. Therefore antitrust laws against cartels in Germany were necessary. I find that our legislation is not sufficiently vigorous along that line.

Big business and concentrated capital should not enjoy certain privileges in taxation. More publicity on the activities of the great capital corporations is needed in order to bring them under the control of public debate and to show the nation how economic power is used. Economic power, like every other form of power in a democratic society, should be exposed to a certain amount of control by public opinion or other institutions. Economic power could easily become political power, especially if this economic power can be used to finance certain political organizations; and therefore the Social Democrats are seeking to pass a law which would make it obligatory for political parties to report the source of their funds.

Germany in her economic policy must of course take account of European cooperation as well as the international scene as a whole. My Social Democratic friend Dr. Heinrich Deist, who died recently, had developed a coherent policy proposal aiming at full employment, a steady growth combined with a stable price level, and — this is the point which marks a difference between the SPD and other parties — a very heavy emphasis on social justice. This point is reflected in income and fiscal policy, in the development of a system of social security and family allocations, in cheap housing, and in other very precise details. In my view, any modern economic policy should make use of economic forecasting. The present government of the Federal Republic did not like that instrument — not until quite recently did the executive branch present to Parliament the first annual economic report with a forecast included. As the Social Democrats have accepted the principle of a market economy, which therefore is not disputed between the SPD and the Christian Democrats, so the Christian Democrats have moved toward the Social Democratic position in the direction of planning. When recently the Christian Democratic members voted in the European parliament for a five-year economic policy for the European institutions, this was a great move forward. The SPD believes that the federation, the states, and the municipal governments have as great a need as business for economic forecasting. The SPD recognizes a responsibility of government for economic health and prosperity.

The modern Federal Republic of Germany has been shaped by the present government and opposition together. The Social Democrats are in power in five states out of eleven. They run most of the large cities, and even in opposition they have had a great influence on legislation. Sometimes their arguments have affected committee action, and sometimes by voting with dissenting members of the government majority they have created a majority against other parts of the government party. I give one example: the field of social security. West Germany has a progressive pension scheme for the aged. They participate every year in the growth of the gross national product, in that pensions are raised according to the rate of progress of the normal standard of living. This has really brightened the prospects of many older people. After ten years of debate, responsibility for family allocations has been transferred to the state, which is the solution the Social Democrats had asked for from the very start. Nearly the whole of the legislation for the victims of political and racial persecution has been pushed through with the impetus of my political friends, although with the help of some very important people in the government, including Chancellor Adenauer. Likewise the legislation for the victims of war, for the reconstruction of the cities, for cheap housing: all has been voted through under heavy pressure by the Social Democrats.

In a similar combination of Social Democratic pressure and cooperation of part of the Christian Democrats, a new welfare device has been created in Germany in the form of what could be translated as "comanagement." It goes farthest in the coal and steel industry but is also used in a less assertive version in the other branches of big industries. The board of managers remains vested with the authority for effective management, as the success of German export efforts has shown. But one of the managers is responsible for all the social problems related to labor, to human relations, to special welfare institutions, and so on. This "welfare director" (*Arbeitsdirektor*) has the full authority of a member of the managing board and can be appointed only with the approval of the workers and employees.

In addition to this, only half the members of the board of directors (*Aufsichtsrat*) to which the management is responsible and which has to make the principal decisions of policy — including distribution of the annual profit between the shareholders, the reserves, social allocations, bonuses to labor, etc. — are elected by the meeting of the shareholders. The other half are elected by labor, and both groups of directors together elect an impartial additional member.

All this has given labor a large influence in the management of the West German coal and steel industry. It has not destroyed the responsibility of management for the policy of the enterprise, but it has given to workers the feeling that they share the responsibility, and this has created a very healthy climate and decreased social conflict and strikes. As the SPD *Basic Programme* states (p. 6): "Freedom and democracy are only thinkable in an industrial society if a constantly growing number of people develop a social consciousness and are ready to help shoulder responsibility."

6

Necessities for the Future

I CAN FAIRLY SAY that the modern Federal Republic of Germany is now far from the capitalism of the nineteenth century and further still from the absolutism that accompanied it in Germany. The Bonn Republic is also more stable than the Weimar Republic. But of course it is far from ideal. I recognize that. Many tasks remain. Let me give some examples of what contemporary Germany needs, as seen through the eyes of a man working for modernization.

MORE EDUCATION

The first necessity, I think, is a crash program for education. Germany lags far behind other industrial nations in that field. If she does not create a better educational system, in a decade or two from now she will not be able to compete inside the Western world against the productivity of other countries. And she will not even be able to compete intellectually with the Eastern world. Therefore there has to be created very soon a system in which all children normally get nine or ten years of compulsory schooling instead of eight. West Germany still has the educational standard the nation had before

1933, and she has not added much capital. This we can see by the number of Nobel Prize winners, which is rather representative of the standard of education in the respective countries. There is a special handicap in the German rural areas, caused by the fact that out of local patriotism and narrow ideological reasons every village tries to keep alive one school with thirty to forty pupils, grouping all the ages together under one teacher. As a group, children in these schools are at a disadvantage whether they attend only for the minimum number of years or try to go on to higher education. I hope more people are coming to feel that we have to regroup our rural school system so that the children in it can be trained and educated in the normal way, with at least one room and one special teacher for every grade.

Fortunately in Germany today teachers (like parents) have learned to think of young people as potential partners, not merely as objects submitted to authority. This new pattern has far-reaching consequences. The new generation feels more independent. There are even critics who claim that not enough authority remains with parents, school, and state. To European tastes, the American system is likely to seem too lenient, but the critical approach of the young generation in Germany to all established authorities is recognized as a positive development for future democracy. As is usually the case in times of transition, some things are overdone. Nevertheless, on the whole, the new German generation is healthily adjusted to the new pattern of society. And the training of teachers has been shaped in a way to encourage that change. Therefore, the young teachers are an especially interesting element of contemporary German society.

This new generation of teachers, together with the very effective influence of press and broadcasting and the continued trials revealing terrible crimes that were committed during the war, have helped to diminish antisemitism in West Germany to an unimportant factor. When signs of antisemitism occur in Germany, the whole world recoils because of the terrible past. But, though the disease has not entirely disappeared, it has been brought under efficient control. In many other countries, antisemitism is now more virulent than in the Federal Republic of Germany, although this does not excuse the past or justify complacency in the present.

Germany needs to raise more students to the high school and college level. In some other industrial countries a stage of education equivalent to two years of college in the United States is reached by more than 13 per cent of the persons of the corresponding age, but the percentage in West Germany is only about 7. (See Table 4.) France, for example, produces 75 per cent more people with that grade of education than the Federal Republic of Germany. Automation, which is on the way to changing a great many economic and social conditions, requires a far greater mobility of people working in certain professions. Twenty years from now, most people will have to master radical changes in their occupation or perhaps change occupations entirely, and this they never can do if they have only a limited intellectual background and then a highly specialized training for a specific job. Once the job of a narrowly trained person

Table 4. Five Countries Compared in Number of Persons Completing Approximate Equivalent of 14 Years' U.S. Schooling [a] in 1950, 1955, 1959, and 1963

Country	Number of persons				As a percentage of those born in the same year			
	1950	1955	1959	1963	1950	1955	1959	1963
France	31,700	40,050	59,100	100,000	4.9	6.8	11.0	16.8
Sweden	5,676	7,478	10,517	16,950	6.4	9.0	11.0	13.7
Netherlands	8,438	8,166	10,029	14,000	5.2	5.2	6.0	7.1
Great Britain	24,600	28,100	36,100	52,400	3.9	4.4	6.0	7.1
Federal Republic of Germany	31,216	31,789	50,454	57,370	4.2	3.7	5.1	7.1

[a] That is, the level of *Abitur* (final examination of the German secondary school); in France *baccalauréat*; in the U.S. through two years of college.

Source: Organization for Economic Cooperation and Development.

ceases to be required, he loses hope of any employment at all.

It is well known that in the United States unemployment is partly a problem of education. People with a good educational background can adjust themselves quickly to a larger variety of professional activities and acquire additional capabilities if required. People lacking this background have great difficulties if technological changes or market conditions make their jobs superfluous. For this reason, unskilled labor is stricken first by unemployment. For the same reason, the colored citizens in the United States suffer more than others from that social disease, because their education still is on the average far behind the normal American standard.

We in Germany have to forecast similar situations in our country and to provide the necessary capacity to adapt to new work requirements. University facilities must be expanded, and ever more research is needed in all fields. This requires more money, more buildings, a change in our system from the grammar school up, and it means especially more training of teachers. It requires the advancement of every gifted child regardless of his social background. Then we shall have achieved mobility in our democratic society; then there will be no more hereditary privileges. The quality of education received today decides the income of tomorrow and determines the social structure of the country the day after tomorrow.

It is crucial that positions of leadership in business, politics, and education not be reserved for a closed circle of families but be accessible to gifted citizens on the basis of performance. This requires a change of attitude at all levels of society. I have often preached to the followers of my party that, if we are striving now for a better country in the future, we must encourage and help our children to seek long-run opportunities. We should not send them too early into a technical job to earn money. Better education is necessary for their future and for the future of the community.

COMMITMENT

One part of every education has to be political education. It is not sufficient to know by heart the text of the constitution. It is necessary to accept responsibilities: this is a moral problem rather than an exercise in learning texts. A nation of nothing but specialists, though well-trained, makes good raw material for dictatorship. Democracy needs democrats, needs citizens who care for the public welfare and the life and future of their community. The citizen must participate in public life between elections. High turn-out at the polls, which we have in Germany, is alone not a sufficient sign of permanent interest and engagement of the citizen. There are far more citizen activities which go beyond defending material group interests in the United States than in West Germany, I have to admit. We still have to develop this kind of grass-roots democracy in Germany. The Social Democratic Party has done good service in that field in an old tradition. With more than 650,000 paying members, nearly three times the membership of the Christian Democrats, the SPD tries to bring participation down to the population. Many people work as volunteers, although noncommitted people look upon these with a kind of contempt, as so-called functionaries. I think this is a degradation of the work of these citizens, who are carrying out an important democratic mission. A living democracy needs this personal engagement. I am quite happy that other parties are now trying also to build this kind of membership for themselves. I wish them success. Such membership is also a basis of financial independence for a party. Political parties need this independence. If it did not exist, pressure groups for limited interests could win too great an influence on parties and legislature. Or the party in power might be tempted to put through a system whereby the state would subsidize out of public funds all the parties represented in Parliament. This would create an undesirable new kind of dependence and inertia. Only if enough citizens voluntarily participate in financing political parties will a proper relation between parties and state power exist.

Another weak point is that a good deal of the German intellectual community is disappointed somewhat with the present political framework. They regret that too much emphasis was laid on the material problems of reconstruction and of economic well-being. This is partly true, but criticism from a distant outsider will not help much. If the moral and intellectual forces of the nation have to be strengthened, our best heads should try to find a better response inside the political context and the political parties and the governmental institutions. But of course responsible political leaders have to meet them half way. We have to create a permanent dialogue between political leadership and intellectual community; better relations between politics, science, and the arts are necessary in Germany. Such a dialogue happens to be part of the tradition of the Social Democrats. They have tried to maintain close ties between intellectual concerns and politics. This was not always the rule, not always successful, but long before 1914 there was a general tendency toward a kind of alliance between intellectuals and the forerunners of the party as it is today.

A time of persecution of the Social Democrats was generally also a time of contempt for the intellectuals outside the sphere of the natural sciences and those fields which were required for technical performance. A critical independent spirit was very often regarded as subversive in German society. It was not understood as a healthy provocation for thought, reflection, and the search for better solutions. During Hitler's regime, the intellectuals were regarded as useful only if they accepted the doctrines of the ruling party identified with the state. No wonder that so many of them left Germany when it was still possible and that many others kept silent during that period.

Unfortunately, a certain habit of regarding the intellectuals as a "ferment of decomposition" (so they were called by the leading Hitlerites) has reappeared over the last decade. This seems to me to have been the result of one party's remaining too long a time in power and identifying itself with the state. Rather than consider whether critical remarks might be justified and whether any reforms might be in order, one important leader went so far as to say that those who were dissatisfied could leave the country. Sometimes, the word "intellectual" was even used with a discriminatory undertone — as if emotions were a better basis for politics than intelligence. This is part of a bad seed from twenty-five years ago which Germany should not cultivate again. After the regrouping of the federal government in 1963, the Christian Democrats became aware of the dangers of such a posture and tried to open a dialogue between some of their leaders and some of the critical elements in the German intellectual community.

This community is not at all identical with the university establishment as such. Arts and literature, on the one side, and the universities, on the other, have not been closely interwoven in Germany. The university establishment was traditionally rather conservative in Germany and largely still is. Before 1933, there was a kind of alliance between the moderate left in political life and the most advanced spirits of the nation, with modern artists, writers, theater directors, and others. Many of them had to leave Germany after Hitler came to power. This was a terrible loss for German cultural life. We have to try to create new bonds between the younger intellectual people and today's politics. These younger people ought to be approached again and again even though they claim they find political life boring. Power and spirit should not be separated. Without a sympathetic relation between the two, both will degenerate. And I dare say this is not restricted to Germany alone.

PLANNING AND PREVENTION

One key problem of West Germany's present and future is the need for long-range city planning (most evident in the case of traffic problems). The Federal Republic of Germany is a small country. Therefore she cannot afford to build new cities in the wilderness: she has no wilderness. But over thirty years, every community renews itself willy-nilly. Therefore, long-range planning can help to shape the future. This is a problem of better coordination of housing, industry, recreation, cultural life, administration, shopping facilities. I think Germany has to organize community facilities better than she did in the past. In fact this is a kind of development policy at home. We should not use this argument against development aid to others; this aid is necessary. But city planning over large areas and over a long period is necessary in Germany and is recognized by the European Communities as a major task even on a European level. A long-range prospect for the future structure of economic, social, and cultural life — urban and rural — has to be developed. Germany (and Europe even more) shows differences in economic standards between the various regions. Certain industries are disappearing. Good housing and education of course attract and produce skilled workers, and industry creates new needs for manpower; therefore we have to look to both things at the same time. All this needs planning over larger areas and a longer time, and we must develop a general concept. This is especially true if we really hope to adjust German agriculture to the growing competition inside the Common Market and to the necessity to carry on trade with the rest of the world. There will be fewer people working in agriculture; therefore we have to organize other jobs and other educational facilities for a part of the rural population in order to get a fair income for this population in the future. Changing patterns of society will not spare agriculture.

Another crucial point is health policy. The Federal Republic of Germany is the Western country with the highest rate of early physical disability. And in all the industrial societies, East and West, there is a growing concern for new dangers to human health. To prevent sickness is surely better than to cure, and a lot can be done in that field. Adding regular checkups to the social security system would help to prevent instead of only to cure or mitigate. We must take a sharp look into the physical conditions of our modern life. Pollution and noise have become a danger to our health and to our nerves. All this needs more observation, more research, and then more action. For example, who should pay to keep an industrial plant from polluting the air? Should it be the community, or should we not ask those who stand to make a profit with their plant to use all the technical facilities which science can offer to prevent other people from getting sick from their business? In this field really we have to do something, and we can. In the larger sense, investment in health pays off by keeping our people able to work.

The fight against pollution and noise will require a lot of public expenditure even if industry can be forced to pay for some of the installations required by its activity. Good water supply, garbage clearance, drainage, modern hospitals, medical care without respect to the financial situation of the person who needs it, research to fight cancer and the diseases of modern civilization — these will claim a bigger share of the public budget than was allotted in the past.

CONSTRUCTIVE OPPOSITION

Germany has taken steps to protect individuals against unemployment, sickness, injury, and the hardships of old age. Now the fight is going on to give ordinary citizens a better share in productive property. Nationalization is not a proper means to that aim. We can exclude also a redistribution of existing property, except through the kind of inheritance tax which is found in nearly all modern countries. The real problem is how to let more people participate in the future growth of the economy. Therefore we have to expand the capacity of the people to save and encourage them to invest what they have saved. This would lead to a greater participation of more people in the growth rate. This is a question of the income policy, but also a question of the policy of the trade unions and the employers in collective bargaining, a question of our fiscal policy and incentives. Social justice should also be the aim of our taxation system. The system now takes too much money through indirect taxation and has not laid enough emphasis on the more justified direct taxation on property and income. A certain reform of the tax scale is pending.

For people from other countries, these main aims of the German Social Democrats will add up to an alternative program, an "opposition." But sometimes in Germany I am asked whether there is an opposition at all. People still hang onto the old conception that the opposition has to offer not an alternative program for government but an alternative set-up for society. Some of them believe that political parties must fight each other from different ideological and philosophical bases as if they were very militant and intolerant religions. But this conception is no longer true. The SPD does not offer another state; it proposes another government for the same state. Germany has now come to a more normal situation for a democratic society. The great parties now have more common ground than they had in the past, and I think that this sharing of common ground — based on the acceptance of the rules of a democratic society, of the constitution, and even of the economic framework — is healthier for the state than the situation before 1933.

The two great parties are becoming more similar in their social structure. Social Democrats are no longer only the party of organized labor; they have won white-collar support. And the Christian Democrats now have a certain support from labor. Therefore the two parties are forced to integrate different group interests inside the party. They cannot defend the interests of one group only, and this makes both parties better able to run the country regardless of which one wins a particular election.

What then are the remaining differences between the parties? The SPD is directed towards a more progressive policy, the Christian Democrats to a more conservative one. Of course this is only a matter of emphasis, but it is visible in daily life. We can fairly assume, for example, that the Federation of German Industry is not quite as sympathetic toward the Social Democrats as toward the

Christian Democrats. That follows from its stand on taxation and other issues. The SPD, on the other hand, finds more sympathy among the leaders of the labor movement, although they claim their independence from the party. The trade unions have Christian Democratic leaders, too. If they are independent from the SPD, that party is also independent from them. The Social Democrats are not just the arm of the unions in the legislature. But a certain affinity still stems from history and from similar outlooks on political and social life.

The decline of ideology in Germany is welcome in that ideological struggle always poses the danger of totalitarianism. In the past the Social Democrats were regarded as outsiders, not able and not willing to run the country even if they had the power to do so. That this feeling has been overcome offers a better prospect for the future of democracy and for peaceful change in government. Some people must be brought to understand that neither the government party nor the opposition party must hold its position in an hereditary way, that they can change their roles. I think this is normal in every democratic state. Sometimes the question is raised what coalition the Social Democrats would be ready to form after the next elections if they did not win a majority of their own. This is a practical problem and not a question of basic principles. It would be unwise for a party to bind its hands before the elections have taken place. We must first ask the electorate and then try to interpret the result. The vote will be difficult enough to analyze. We have to admit that in a democratic pattern of society, if there is not a clear-cut majority for one party alone, all democratic parties must be regarded as possible partners, and none should be excluded from that possibility.

In foreign policy, the margin for German maneuvering is rather narrow. This has already been explained in previous chapters. It is clear that both parties now more or less agree on the need for European integration and Atlantic solidarity. Some critics say: "Well, here one can see that there are no differences between parties. There is no opposition!" Opposition does not necessarily look for foreign-policy issues in order to compete for power. Domestic issues serve quite as well.

PEACEFUL REVOLUTION

Democracy sometimes appears dull. It needs a daily effort. Changes are made step by step and not by revolutions, but these changes involve every citizen and need his participation. To say that responsibility lies with the citizen, however, is not to deny that democracy also needs leadership. The leadership in government or in a party must fight for consensus. The leaders must fight for approval of their ideas and convictions. If the leadership can be changed, it cannot dictate an opinion. It must convince. At the same time, let us understand that leadership should not just follow public-opinion polls. If a leadership breaks down to that, then a nation is behaving like a leaf in the wind. Leadership has to shape public opinion, to try to have an influence on it, not by unfair means but by speaking out. Leaders must develop convictions of their own on what is right, what is necessary, and what is possible, and then fight for these convictions in the framework of the party and in the framework of the nation. If this did not take place, there would be no leadership at all, and democracy would not survive. Democracy can survive only if the virtues of leadership also exist; but it is leadership for a prescribed period only, and the quality of performance determines whether the mandate will be renewed or not. Opinion polls are necessary to suggest the mood and concerns of the nation but not to show what is right.

Furthermore, democracy needs inspiration, especially if it is to attract the younger generation. They do not want to be consumers only. An appeal to the creative spirit of our young people is necessary. We strive for creating a better society in our own country. We have also to create adequate instruments for a better relationship between countries, to create larger communities, whether an integrated Europe, the Atlantic community, or even the United Nations. The speed of technical development in recent times, which will become even greater in the future, forces us to adapt our political institutions to change. If not, mankind will be destroyed by its own creations. War can no longer be conceived as a great adventure. Even though we must be able to fight if necessary in order to avoid slavery, and this capability may preserve peace, what is before us in the future is the real adventure of shaping our future with all the immense facilities the human race has acquired. This gigantic task will require such an amount of research and imagination, of action and courage, of foresight and will, that the best brains will be needed. This task will not be achieved or accomplished unless dedicated young people work hard in their own countries and others to do all the things which have to be done in modernizing state and society and in helping other nations in the world to reach a high standard. A peaceful revolution may be in the offing, a fascinating experience — if leadership in all the great countries in the world can avoid the destruction of our civilization by World War III or by anarchy following from a failure to deal with the burning needs of the developing countries. Is this not an adventure worth living for?

⇢⟫ **7** ⟪⇠

Conclusion

THERE IS A TRADITIONAL English definition of democracy: democracy is government by discussion. We have to add something. Once discussion ends, as it must, then a decision has to be taken, either by the citizens acting in common or by their representatives. Direct democracy is seldom as feasible for large states as it is for the Swiss, who decide even minor items by plebiscite if the issue is clear and if real alternatives exist. We others, and the Swiss too in many cases, do it by representation. We make a decision on the team that will run the country; we select the government. We do this by our free elections.

They are free only if there is also freedom of opinion. We know that the elected government has to be responsible to the electorate because in a free society this electorate is, as the Swiss say, the "sovereign." Inherent in the character of a democratic state is the possibility of change, of peaceful change — change by the ballot, change by election. To provide for free discussion and orderly change, we have to create all the necessary safeguards which have been developed over centuries, step by step, sometimes by hard fights, by revolutions, by civil wars, sometimes only by normal development. Thus in the Western world we have created an open society — open for new men, open for new ideas, open for competition for leadership between men and parties inside our states. And we have devised separation of power to protect the freedom of the citizen. The legislative, executive, and judicial powers are never concentrated in one hand, and we give the "sovereign" ways of controlling officials during their time of office as well as at election time. The existence of different parties is a protection of the citizen, too, against misuses of power. In the United States all this is called the system of checks and balances, but some form of it is found in every democratic nation, and it leads to a dynamic society. I say dynamic because democracy is never achieved once and for all. It remains always a task in every nation. There are chances and dangers in every nation. Individuals are good and bad, and most are somewhere in between. There is no such thing as a permanent invariable character of a nation, neither in Germany nor elsewhere.

Vigilance is necessary everywhere and all the time. Democracy can exist only if its institutions adapt to the necessities of the times. Democracy must live and cannot stand still. It requires the cooperation of its citizens. If they indulge in private life only and neglect their participation in the democratic process of discussion and decision, they will lose their freedom, either to more or less benevolent bureaucracies or to reckless minorities. Individuals can learn; nations are influenced by experience. The catastrophe of the Hitler regime and the establishment of a totalitarian Communist regime in one part of Germany have led the overwhelming majority of Germans to see the consequences of their own dreadful past.

There are still some ghosts of the past. I regret that the government did not refuse from the very start to appoint people to public positions who could only create misunderstanding and open possibilities for Communist propaganda against Germany. But the Weimar Republic lasted only fourteen years. Twenty years have passed since Germany lay in ruins in 1945. The ghosts are not in power. They try to survive in the shelter of the new democratic regime. The most important ones have been eliminated, and they have been partly eliminated by the pressure of public opinion. This is a sign of democratic strength and vigor. Some still continue to serve. The most patriotic thing they could do is retire, but they are not a danger.

A bit of self-confidence among the democratic forces is also a necessity. If democracy in Germany should be threatened now, the threat would stem not from the forces of the past but from new mistakes and new errors.

There is one new problem that needs some observation. This is the possible revival of nationalism in Germany by an infection coming this time from France. German-French reconciliation is one of the greatest achievements following World War II. It was not initiated by De Gaulle, but he joined it, and I am glad of that. Reconciliation is in the old tradition of the European social democratic parties. Socialists used to be regarded by the nationalist forces in their countries as traitors, just because of their attempt to reconcile France and Germany. Persecution and assassination of such men as Jean Jaurès proved that. I am happy that now the right wing of public opinion in both our countries has joined the movement. But German-French relations should not be regarded as a kind of separate bloc excluding and opposing others. The Bundestag, at the request of my party — and I drafted a good deal of the resolution — made a preamble to the German-French treaty saying that we regard this very close relationship as part of the European Community in the spirit of Atlantic solidarity, not as a pact outside or against these common institutions. There can be no European Community without France, but there can also be no European defense without the United States. I think we should not attempt to pool former nationalisms and now to bring them together in the same nationalist spirit to form a common nationalism for two or for six countries. We have to overcome narrow nationalism. Europe should be open to the world and not a closed shop.

The Europeans, especially the Germans and the French, should not overestimate their national capabilities. In the past this has happened, and we have paid for it. It should not happen to both countries together now. When in 1941 a certain young German officer was sent to the front, he took leave from his mother in a room where there was a great map of the world. The mother asked him: "Where is Russia? I hear our troops have gone there." And the son answered: "Here, look, a sixth of the globe." Then she asked, "And where is the United States?" — because, in his wisdom, Hitler had also declared war on the United States. The mother was shown the United States. "We're at war with England, too," she said. "Show me the British Empire." The son pointed out Great Britain, Canada, most of Africa, India, Pakistan, Ceylon, Burma, Australia, New Zealand. And then the mother at the end asked: "Now, where is Germany?" He showed her the little place on the map. "Tell me," she said, "does Hitler know this too?"

I think we should tell this story again and again to ourselves and even from time to time to our French neighbors. France and Germany together are stronger than they would be alone, but even together they are no world power in these days. Clear knowledge of the power situation and of the dreadful consequences of disregarding it is necessary. A very good old French saying, *On ne peut faire que la politique de ses moyens*, lets us know that our policy cannot be more grandiose than the means at our disposal. Let us be vigilant enough to recognize in time what we have to do. Democracy is not protected merely by maintaining a negative position toward its opponents. It gains strength in solving current problems and by mobilizing citizens for the public welfare. Democracy is achieved not by aspirations but by performance.

Now we come back to the questions raised in the first chapter of this book. Has the world good cause to believe that a Hitler-type regime will return in Germany? Or do the remnants of authoritarianism represent a diminishing part of the dreadful past in Germany's present, more than compensated for by institutions, ideas, men, and forces working for the good cause?

Without neglecting existing dangers and problems, I

personally share the second view. Suspicious incidents on which Americans base their questions do sometimes take place. But they do not indicate a comeback of past times. They show that not all the traces of a dreadful past have disappeared in Germany. They represent the last futile spasms of the old order. We had a debate in Germany about the need for further trials of people involved in the operation of concentration camps, trials which attract world-wide attention. We, and our young people especially, think they are needed because we have to bring these things before our own courts, in order not to give the impression that Germans do not want to hear those things and are content to leave such matters to others. Sometimes the sentences handed down at these trials are unsatisfactory, we recognize, but at least they bring out the truth from a dark chapter of German history. There is great value in telling the truth and educating the younger generation so that such things may never happen again in their country. I know that these trials come late. It was not easy to bring together the evidence, and some witnesses have disappeared. The Allies withheld their documents for many years. The Communists reveal cases only when it suits them for propaganda purposes. If they had been really interested in clearing the atmosphere forever, they would have published all the files they had or handed copies of the whole material to the German federal authorities. They did not choose to — partly because they prefer to fire carefully selected shots from time to time in order to create a permanent climate of mistrust and to misrepresent the Federal Republic of Germany as the political heir to the Hitler regime. They know that this is not true. But they hope that their reckless propaganda might have results over a longer period.

It is regrettable that nearly every new publication from the old files leads to the discovery of a man in a profession or career he should not be in, with such a past. Had the documents been laid on the table years ago, action would have been possible. Sometimes no legal action is possible at all — if the man is not in an official position and if his deeds are already sanctioned by an Allied court. The old rule of *ne bis in idem*, that nobody can be sentenced twice for the same crime, has to be applied also in these cases. Some say, "Why do you give fair treatment to those people? Do they really merit it?" I reply that in a state ruled by law no verdict can be delivered without proof. This we stood for against Hitler, and this we must stand for even now. This is one of the principles we have to defend at home and in the Alliance.

The catastrophic consequences of two totalitarian regimes for the nation, the more recent solidarity with the Western democracies, and the rebuilding of the country in a democratic framework have had a great impact on public opinion. As education passes over into the hands of a new generation of educators, the roots of democracy will grow even deeper. If there are dangers, they do not come from the past. A certain longing for the "strong man" in place of parliamentary democracy comes this time from our western neighbor. Nationalist infection, sometimes covered by a pan-European phraseology, goes together with a certain admiration for a new authoritarian style of government. We must remember that as

time strengthens the normal democratic base by education, it also puts a greater distance between the new generation and World War II — and therefore diminishing
the war's immunizing effect. Each generation has to work
for democracy. In Germany, democracy has been created
in close cooperation with our Western friends. Those
who risk that friendship, in Germany and elsewhere, are
weakening democracy in Germany.

The way in which our Allies, mainly the U.S., deal with
the problems of our country, will have an important impact on our common future. If Western solidarity maintains a proper environment for Germany's political and
economic well-being in the world of today, if that solidarity proves to be the best method to secure peace and
freedom, to develop a society based on the dignity of
man and on justice in the political and social field, and
to defend the legitimate interests of the nation, then I
have no fear. But if we again become strangers to each
other, if suspicion is nourished and destroys confidence,
the old evils of isolation might reappear. In our modern
age, democracy must promote cooperation among nations
even more than in the past. We in Germany have the
largest part of the work to do, but the behavior of others
also has a certain part in the outcome of the struggle for
democracy in Germany.

Index